UNDERSTANDING
CRIME
and
DELINQUENCY

a sociological introduction

Michael Phillipson

ALDINE PUBLISHING COMPANY - CHICAGO

ABOUT THE AUTHOR

Michael Phillipson received his B.A. in 1961 and his M.A. by
thesis in 1964 from the University of Nottingham. He has
held several research posts in the past ten years, including
one in the Social Medicine Research Unit Study of Delinquency
and another in the Political and Economic Planning Data
Archives Feasibility Study. He is presently Senior Lecturer
in Sociology at the University of London, Goldsmiths College.

This book is a substantially revised edition of a work
first published in Great Britain under the title of
Sociological Aspects of Crime and Delinquency.

Aldine Publishing Company
529 South Wabash Avenue
Chicago, Illinois 60605

ISBN 0–202–23141–0 clothbound edition
    0–202–23142–9 paperbound edition
Library of Congress Catalog Number 73–84934

Printed in the United States of America

We beg delinquents for our life.
Behind each bush perhaps a knife;
each landscaped crag, each flowering shrub
hides a policeman with a club.

—Robert Lowell, "Central Park"

Contents

Foreword

During the past decade, the traditional approach to understanding crime and delinquency has come in for increasing criticism. This approach assumes that the law and legal agents identify crime and delinquency, criminals and delinquents. Its tasks are, first, to find the reasons why some persons and not others engage in crime and delinquency, and second, to assess the means purported to deter persons from engaging in crime and delinquency in the first place or again. In addressing the first task a search is made for the features of persons and settings that differentiate those who do from those who do not engage in crime and delinquency. In attempting to fulfill the second task, the capacity of various ways to change these features is evaluated.

Most texts dealing with crime and delinquency, criminals and delinquents, take this approach to the subject matter. It is difficult not to do so. These are or seem to be eminently practical questions, well worth answering, and there is considerable pressure to work toward answers for them—scholarship in this field, as in others, not being quite so "ivory tower" as is sometimes assumed or wished. Further, the overwhelming bulk of research in the field implicitly or explicitly aims to answer one or both of the traditional questions. Finally, untraditional approaches are only now being articulated, criticism of the traditional having outstripped any substitute for it.

In any event, most texts continue to approach crime and delinquency traditionally, even though their authors are aware, often painfully aware, of the many difficulties involved. This can be seen in both the organization of texts and in what is considered worthy of extended analysis. Thus, we normally find that:

First, various forms of crime and delinquency as found in the law are outlined. The point of this exercise seems to be to familiarize the presumably naive reader with statutory law and the acts with which the law deals. There is nothing wrong with this objective, in my view at least. What is troubling is, that by and large, that ends the matter. How the law got the way it is; how it changes; how it is related to other normative efforts; the degree of conflict and consensus underlying the law; the relation of the law to the day-to-day activities of those charged with interpreting and implementing it—none of these matters is ordinarily discussed. Of course, one cannot do everything. But one major criticism of the traditional approach to crime and delinquency is that it takes its own central subject matter for granted. One might say that the core is left unexplored in a rush to examine the periphery.

Second, after outlining the law and the various forms of illegal activities, the distributions of these activities are suggested. Here the object seems to be to show that different proportions of persons of different ages, sex, socioeconomic status, and ethnic identification engage in illegal actions, at least as measured by official counts. It is duly noted that these counts are not very trustworthy and increasingly unofficial counts—self-reports, victim surveys— are used as supplements. Then various theories are assessed for their utility in accounting for these distributions. The outcome of this effort, typically, is to show that theories other than the one entertained by the author have critical defects and that the author's theory, if he has one, does a better job of accounting for what he finds interesting about what is known—but that it, too, requires further testing.

And third, the criminal justice apparatus is described, often critically. Lengthy discussion of this apparatus is a rather new feature of texts in "criminology" and probably represents in itself some erosion of the traditional approach. The main point of most current textual presentations remains arguably traditional, however, their point being to evaluate the capacity of criminal justice agencies and programs to deter crime and delinquency. The main conclusion seems to be that little, if any, deterrence takes place, if this is measured by rearrests. Whether or not law and legal agencies deter persons from engaging in criminal and delinquent acts in the first place continues to be hotly debated.

Understanding Crime and Delinquency is intended to help introduce readers to a different approach to the subject. This approach invokes a sociological framework and makes use of comparative materials; Michael Phillipson calls it—for want, at the moment, of some more widely used term—the "interactionist perspective." Phillipson does not insist that this is the only perspective that may usefully be adopted by those concerned with crime and delinquency. Indeed, although he is critical of the traditional approach, he does not claim it is worthless. He is more interested, happily, in describing the ways in which the interactionist perspective may open avenues for inquiry that help us better grasp how criminal and delinquent phenomena take place in the world, and how the analysis of these phenomena can bring insight into our day-to-day lives.

Phillipson invokes a sociological framework because of

his interest in crime and delinquency as social events, and because of his belief that analysis of these events provides a powerful vehicle for exploring processes and structures that pervade social life more generally. Crime and delinquency can be and, indeed, usually have been analyzed with other ends in view. Sometimes these ends have been mainly practical, as in the traditional approach. Sometimes they have been theoretical, it being quite possible, for example, to be interested in crime and delinquency as psychic rather than social events, and in their analysis as a means of learning more about psychic processes and structures. Phillipson is not arguing, as I understand him, with those who would take a practical approach or with those who prefer some other theoretical framework. He is arguing against confusing the practical with the theoretical, and with lack of clarity about which theoretical framework is being adopted. He is mainly extending an invitation to understand crime and delinquency as social events, as happenings that involve exchanges between persons. Another part of the invitation is to try to generalize from these to other exchanges. Put differently, by looking closely at crime and delinquency we can enlarge our understanding of how we collectively produce stability and change in the social world.

In this enterprise, the author of *Understanding Crime and Delinquency* is hesitant to draw many firm generalizations. In part this seems to result from what he terms a "dialectical response" to the traditional approach, which abounds with generalizations most of which are weakly if at all supported by reliable and valid data. In part also, Phillipson seems moved to hesitancy by his sense that comparative materials should be consulted before general statements are set forth. Readers will find this volume much more useful than most in suggesting how comparative materials suggest both caution and the necessity and correctness of continuing to press for properly qualified generalizations.

As noted, *Understanding Crime and Delinquency* takes an "interactionist perspective" on crime and delinquency. I shall not try to outline the perspective here; most of the volume is devoted to this task. It is perhaps proper to say that I believe this perspective extremely useful in helping one shake loose from the traditional view and to appreciate that other questions can be asked which are worth pursuing with vigor. The interactionist perspective puts the views of the actors in social life front and center as topics for analysis, challenging the analyst to articulate the assumptions about the world implicit in these views. This is especially useful in the study of crime and delinquency. The views of the actors engaged in these activities are crucial, particularly when "views" (like "perspectives" or "labels") are seen as embodied in the ways we deal with each other—not simply, or even mainly, in how we "see" or what we "call" each other. Further, it is Phillipson's contention, with which I agree, that the views of the actors in the social events of crime and delinquency are similar in most respects to the views of traditional criminologists. Understanding one is most helpful in understanding the values and limits of the other.

It follows that the interactionist perspective directs attention to what persons do in the world—how they make it through the day, the kinds of cooperative and conflicting activities they attempt to sustain, and the resources they are able to bring to these activities. Social life as it is lived, and the facilities and constraints that affect it, are the true subject of understanding from the interactionist perspective, as they are for all sociology. Studying crime and delinquency is one excellent way to enter into this complicated, probably inexhaustible subject. In particular, crime and delinquency help us appreciate the character of the occasions when we create trouble for each other; what leads us to consider some kinds of trouble and trouble-makers more important than others; and what, collectively, we choose to do about all these things. These are no small matters. *Understanding Crime and Delinquency,* by Michael Phillipson, will help any reader understand that this is so and how, through study, he can understand more.

Sheldon L. Messinger

Preface

The original version of this book was written to offer English students a reasonably systematic introduction to an interactionist perspective on crime and delinquency and to place a sociological understanding of it in the wider context of social deviance. I felt that there was a need to draw together some of the main ideas that had informed the analysis of deviance over the previous decade and to show how these reflected some fairly dramatic changes in the emphases and mood of sociologists of deviance. These changes, both in ways of thinking about deviance and in those aspects of the phenomenon that were seen as setting the basic problems for analysis, were sufficiently radical to set the emerging work in direct contrast to much that had preceded it.

The interactionist perspective provides for a fairly clean break with some of the founding assumptions of most earlier work on deviance in general and crime and delinquency in particular. It is for this reason that I feel justified in adopting a highly critical stance to what I term "traditional criminology" (I include within this much of the earlier sociological work on crime) and drawing a clear line between traditional perspectives and contemporary developments. By extension, I have spent little space giving detailed criticisms of this earlier work, preferring to present the interactionist perspective as a relatively inde-

UNDERSTANDING CRIME AND DELINQUENCY

pendent and internally consistent standpoint. I do not wish to suggest, of course, that the interactionist perspective has no continuities in personnel or affinities (in, say, the use of certain concepts) with its predecessors. It would, I think, be more accurate to see the work of the interactionists as a dialectical response to intractable problems faced in traditional work; in a sense, the interactionist perspective gains much of its strength and attraction from the fact that it can be seen as a response called forth by the failures of previous analysis to solve some fundamental problems.

It provides a neat illustration within sociology of what Kuhn (1970) refers to as a "paradigm revolution" in the natural sciences. A paradigm (the constellation of beliefs, values, and techniques shared by the members of a given scientific community) defines both the "normal" scientific puzzles of the scientific community and the ways of solving them; crises emerge in normal science when anomalies or discrepancies in the fit between theory and nature are seen as insoluble within the constraints of the operative paradigm. A crisis is solved by the adoption of an alternative paradigm within which the anomaly can be more adequately dealt with:

> The decision to reject one paradigm is simultaneously the decision to accept another, and the judgment leading to that decision involves the comparison of both paradigms with nature and with each other (Kuhn, 1970, p. 77).

and similarly:

> Just because the emergence of a new theory breaks with one tradition of scientific practice and introduces a new one conducted under different rules and within a different universe of discourse, it is likely to occur only when the first tradition is felt to have gone badly astray (p. 86).

The questions asked, the methods employed, and the interpretations offered within the interactionist perspective on crime are the outcome of a paradigm revolution within the sociological investigation of crime.

However, the very occurrences of paradigm shifts or revolutions should sensitize us to the impermanence of paradigms; the advantages of the interactionist perspective over previous orientations should not blind us to the inevitability of its own eventual demise. Rather than seeing it as providing the only answers to our questions about deviance, we should be well advised to treat it as a useful advance on earlier thinking. In terms of its own assumptions, methods, and concepts, it remains inevitably a partial and selective perspective on deviance (indeed this "selective" characteristic is a defining feature of the very idea of a "perspective"). Added point is given to this warning about treating the interactionist perspective as the definitive orientation toward deviance by noting another contemporary development in general sociology.

The emergence of an approach to sociology firmly grounded in phenomenology and linguistic philosophy is also illustrative of a paradigm revolution in sociology in which the emerging approach suspends the relevance of the assumptions, methods and concepts of most sociology to its own analytical problems (see Garfinkel, 1967; Cicourel, 1964; Douglas, 1970a; Sudnow, 1972; Schuetz, 1967; Filmer et al, 1972). This is clearly not the place to formulate the problems and policies of this phenomenologically grounded sociology, but it is worth noting that the interactionist perspective has strong affinities with this new movement through, for example, their common concern with the processual character of social life. The interactionist perspective might develop most fruitfully through its proponents paying close attention to the recommendations and styles of analysis of the phenomenological sociologists.

Although deviance per se is not a fundamental substantive interest of the writers in this emergent perspective, by a fortunate coincidence several such sociologists have studied contexts of direct relevance in the analysis of deviance to illustrate their theoretical concerns. Most of this work extends our understanding through its substantive focus on some of the very issues so strongly emphasized in the interactionist perspective—namely those centering on societal reaction to and social control of deviance. As a result of their detailed interest in the methodic procedures members employ in producing and sustaining an intelligible world, ethnomethodologists have coincidentally produced a series of relevant descriptions showing how the "work" in a variety of social control settings gets done. Their studies of police work (Bittner, 1967), court work (Sudnow, 1965), institutional culture (Wieder, 1969), and the recognition of deviance (Blum, 1970) give clear directives for the future development of research into deviance by displaying the sociological gains possible from careful observation of the mundane and "unquestioned" practices that constitute societal reactions to deviance.

In preparing this book for American readers I have tried to display the values of a comparative perspective on crime by retaining references to English material where this seemed appropriate. This exemplifies a main tenet of the interactionist perspective, namely that the patterns of deviance and control are relative to time and place; comparing our own cultural patterns and experiences with those of other cultures helps us to guard against facile analytical or moral judgments about the phenomena studied. At the same time, we hope it helps us to distinguish that which is particular to our culture and differentiates it from others, from those putatively general phenomena which lock us into the human community.

I am indebted to Sheldon L. Messinger for his valuable comments, assistance and encouragement in my revision of this book for publication in the United States. I would also like to thank Mel Pollner for his helpful suggestions. Needless to say, I alone am responsible for the text that follows.

I

Introduction:
Some Problems of
Traditional Criminology

Introduction

The sociological study of crime and delinquency raises issues that are of general importance to the discipline of sociology. These issues concern the kinds of questions sociologists ask, the kinds of methods of investigation they use and the kinds of explanations or interpretations they offer. One issue in particular is well illustrated by the sociological analysis of crime, and it is an issue that underlies the main arguments of this book. The fact that crime is viewed as an important social problem by some members of society raises the complex issue of the nature of the relationship between sociological "knowledge" and problems and those things defined as social problems by the members of society in their everyday practical thinking. Can a distinction be made between sociological problems and social problems? If so, what is the relationship between the two? An underlying theme of this book is that such a distinction can and should be made and that making it has direct implications for the questions sociologists ask about the phenomenon of crime. The discussion rests, to a great extent, on the contrast that is drawn between traditional criminology and the contemporary sociological study of

1

crime and delinquency. Traditional criminology, with its
European origins, grew out of and rested on disciplines
other than sociology (medicine, psychiatry, law), and their
interests left an indelible mark on the character of criminology's development. A concern of this book is to hasten
the move away from these origins toward more truly sociological analyses of crime. That such an exhortation to
sociologists to move away from the nonsociological concerns of traditional criminology is still necessary is a
comment on the extent of the influence of earlier criminological ways of thinking on the development of the sociology of crime and delinquency. A comparison of earlier
criminology and the developing sociology of crime illustrates both the peculiar difficulties involved in the social
scientific analysis of crime and also some of the ways in
which the social scientists have tried to justify their claims
to scientific status.

In the following discussion I distinguish between sociological and criminological studies of crime done from
more traditional viewpoints and an emergent viewpoint
that I shall refer to as an "interactionist" perspective and
which is elaborated in the next chapter. Crime is, of course,
studied by disciplines other than sociology, but in this book
my concern is with issues in the *sociological* study of crime
and the ways in which these relate to general problems of
theorizing and researching in sociology and their social
utilization. The term *criminology,* then, as it is used in the
rest of the book, while necessarily referring to work done
in other disciplines such as law and psychology, includes
most sociological studies of crime and delinquency up to
the emergence of the interactionist perspective. In this
chapter I argue that most "academic" study of crime and
delinquency, including most sociological writing until very
recently, has tended to accept and work within the terms
of "official" assumptions regarding the character of crime

and criminals, rather than and analyzing the very assumptions themselves. Moreover, most of this work has been done within a positivistic frame of reference which typically dehumanizes man by reducing him to an *object* of study; in doing this the work covers its own value commitments by laying spurious claims to scientific status.

Criminology's subject matter

Students of crime, like other students who take social political, practical, or moral problems as their subject matter, face peculiar difficulties if they also wish to claim scientific status for their work. Criminology does not focus on one level of behavior but nevertheless attempts to provide explanations of particular forms of behavior, namely, criminal actions; as its subject matter is limited to highly particular forms of socially defined behavior (crime), its theories and its methods are forced into the position of having to apply every level of analysis (chemical, physiological, psychological, and sociological) to the phenomena that it is trying to understand. There are many problems that stem from this approach and make the validity of criminological explanations difficult to accept. Because criminologists are often aware of the difficulties of validating their claims to provide explanations, they have to develop a rationale and justification for their activities; such a rationale has to be more than simply the interest in the drama of crime that they share with many other members of society. The criminological rationale is provided by the fact that crime in industrial societies is defined as a serious social and political problem, and the hope is that analysis of this social problem by criminologists could lead to more effective ways of dealing with it. However, the way that this rationale has been interpreted in traditional criminology raises crucial questions about its pretensions to certain kinds of objectivity and criminologists' claims to scientific status for their work. In this chapter, the most fundamental of the analytical problems that face criminology are discussed briefly as a prolegomenon to the presentation of an alternative sociological perspective for the analysis of crime.

From a contemporary sociological perspective, the short history of criminology can be read as a history of failure, and it is a failure to which sociologists themselves have made a considerable contribution. An understanding of this failure requires a critique of the kinds of questions asked by criminologists, the ways in which they try to answer them and the assumptions upon which criminology rests. Criminology, like other scientific disciplines, makes claims to objectivity, and yet it differs in one crucial respect from the other sciences: it is probably the only discipline whose subject matter is defined not by its own intrinsic qualities but by society at large and by those groups with authority in particular.

The scientist, whether natural or social, normally has the freedom to create and define his own terms, such definitions in themselves limiting his field of study. His definitions may undergo constant change in a rapidly developing science, but the changes arise out of the scientist's theories and research and not by external fiat; certainly particular interest groups in society, such as industrial or governmental, do attempt to control the direction of scientific research, but they cannot define its limiting concepts. Thus, while the area of the scientist's research can always be viewed as the product of the interplay of a range of values (stemming from the scientist himself, the scientific community, industry and government), during the course of his research the scientist's questions arise from the interests of his particular discipline and the nature of the phenomena with which it is concerned. His choice of certain styles of theories, concepts and methods, which actually define the limits of his studies, arises out of the concerns of the discipline and the criteria used within it to evaluate his work.

The basic difference between criminology (as it developed in the European and largely nonsociological context) and other scientific disciplines is that the criminologist has his subject matter defined for him by noncriminologists; other people place the limits on his discipline. Very simply, criminology is the study of crime and the criminal; however, the sorts of behavior defined as crime and those individuals convicted as criminal emerge out of social processes quite independent of the activities of professional criminologists. Criminal behavior is defined by the criminal law, and law is created through a range of elaborate social processes within the political and legal institutions of industrial societies. Similarly, it is through such institutions that we set up, maintain and sometimes change the penal institutions that deal with the people who are convicted of breaking the criminal law. The criminologist thus has his subject matter given him by the society through its formal definitions of illegal behaviors—crime—and its identification of some of the people who commit criminal acts— the convicted criminals.

A recognition that the creation of the criminal law in contemporary industrial societies is a process of political conflict and compromise and that the penal system is only able to select out a proportion of all those who break the law, reveals three facts that have important implications for the explicit goals of criminology. The legal definition of what is criminal behavior changes within any society (for example, the recent changes in England in the law relating to homosexual behavior) and in the United States, changes in court interpretations about pornographic literature and movies, and about indecent conduct. Different societies have different definitions of what is criminal be-

havior (for example, many forms of gambling and drug use
which are quite legal in England and elsewhere are criminal offences in most of the United States). Societies' reactions to crime, expressed in their penal apparatus and the
institutions that "back up" the law, change according to
time and place (for example, the abolition of the death
penalty or changes in the ways in which prisons are used).
This temporal and cultural relativity in relation to the social definitions of and the responses to crime mean that
there is no one behavioral entity we can call crime; there
is no behavior that is always and everywhere criminal. This
crucial fact lies at the basis of the present criticism of criminology and is central to the subsequent discussion of sociological perspectives on crime and delinquency. Crime
and the criminal result from social definitions and social
processes. The study of crime and the criminal, therefore,
makes criminology a "normative" discipline—that is, one
that rests initially on the evaluation by noncriminologists
of what "the problem" is; its subject matter is defined by
particular social values. The intellectual space within
which criminologists work is mapped out and delineated by
the everyday activities and concerns of others.

Criminologists prefer to reject the suggestion that their
discipline is normative (see, for example, Mannheim, 1965,
I, p. 13) by asserting that the objective study of norms is
not in itself normative. However, it seems possible to demonstrate criminology's normative character by showing
how far its acceptance of the legal and social definitions of
crime and the criminal limits its objectivity and precludes
its achievement of its stated goals of explanation.

Criminology's aims and claims

If the criminologist has his subject matter defined for him
through social processes unrelated to scientific analysis,

how does this impinge on the questions he asks and the answers he obtains? The central concern of criminology has been and still is (Mannheim, 1965; Walker, 1967; S. and E. Glueck, 1964) to locate "the causes of crime." This stated aim is very often accompanied by explicit and implicit suggestions that once we have located these "causes" we can do something about "the problem" in the form of "treatment" or "prevention" (Mannheim, 1965, I, p. 20; Walker, 1967, p. 17). Thus, complementary to the search for "causes" in criminology has been an interest in the reform, rehabilitation, change and control of the criminal. For example, criminologists have been very much concerned with the problem of evaluating the different penal sentences; evaluation here refers to attempts to measure the success of penal sentences in reducing levels of recidivism or re-offending among convicted offenders (Glaser, 1964; Mannheim and Wilkins, 1955). The two major areas of theory and research in criminology, then, are crime causation and the "treatment" of offenders; the aims are to find "the causes" and to improve "treatment."

Seen from the sociological perspective we will outline, these aims and concerns of criminology are inappropriate because they are based both upon false assumptions about the nature of crime and the criminal and also upon implicit, and sometimes explicit, prescriptions about what society *should* do in relation to crime and delinquency; such value prescriptions are in themselves an immediate denial of criminologists' claims to scientific impartiality and objectivity. A brief examination of these assumptions may help to clarify the case against traditional criminology and also suggest more appropriate perspectives for an analysis of crime and delinquency.

The key defining feature of criminology is that the criminal law is accepted as a given and becomes, therefore, the defining and limiting criterion of the discipline. In practice this has meant that criminologists have almost entirely ignored the study of the social processes by which the criminal law is made and changed (an exception to this is Jerome Hall, "Theft, Law and Society," 1939), of the values on which it rests and their distribution in society, of the processes by which law is maintained and enforced and of the complex relationship between societal reactions to crime in the shape of the penal system and the quantity and quality of crime in a society. Failure to ask such questions about the criminal law and the values and processes on which it is based means that criminology rests upon an implicit acceptance of the legal "status quo;" this is, in itself a value position and a surrender of the criminologists' claim to objectivity. This unquestioning acceptance of the values upheld by the criminal law seriously limits the type of questions criminologists ask and also the answers they obtain to questions concerning, for example, "the causes of crime." In practice, this has resulted in criminologists restricting their focus in the search for "causes" almost entirely to individuals officially convicted of criminal offenses. Perhaps this limited vision and the unwillingness to question the legal process is unsurprising in view of the fact that criminologists have traditionally been drawn largely from two of the most conservative professional groups—the law and medicine. The law seems designed to protect many of their interests. It is difficult for such groups to undertake disinterested research into some of the very values on which their social status rests. The basic premise of traditional criminology and much sociology seems to have been, therefore, that it is possible to locate "the causes of crime" by a study of the convicted criminal population.

The protagonists of this approach attempt to locate these "causes" through the application, in principle, of natural scientific models of explanation and methods of measurement. The debate between proponents of the natural scientific approach (positivism or determinism) and the "free will" approach (voluntarism or intentionalism) continues in sociology and concerns disagreements as to the most appropriate perspective and methods for the analysis of social life; in criminology, however, the argument seems to have been decided, with very little debate, firmly in favor of positivism. In simple terms the criminological positivist argues that there are underlying causes for every criminal act and that his job is to define, find and measure them; he believes that there is an underlying pattern of events or factors historically antecedent to the criminal act which is its cause. This pattern of events is what the natural scientist calls the necessary and sufficient conditions for the occurrence of any given phenomenon. The criminologist is thus trying to find the laws according to which this pattern of conditions necessary and sufficient for criminal behavior operates. In fact, most of these criminologists who have applied this approach to criminal behavior seem to have assumed that the acts of the convicted criminals could be explained by focusing on the convicted criminals alone and without reference to the encompassing social processes. The assumption is that "the causes" can be found by an examination of convicted criminals' personal biographies and that the necessary and sufficient conditions for the commission of and conviction for a criminal act are located within these personal biographies.

The methodology of traditional criminology appears to equate noncriminality with nonconviction; failure to investigate the methods by which society produces a population of officially known and labeled criminals requires criminologists to assume that these officially known offenders are a representative sample of all criminal rule breakers. They wish to locate the causes of crime *in general* but go about this task by researching the biographies of only the officially convicted population; they generalize from official criminals to crime in general. Assumptions about the differences between criminals and non-criminals have resulted in the predominance of certain kinds of methods in criminology; in particular, there has been much use of the comparison of samples of convicted delinquents or criminals with control groups of nondelinquents matched on a limited range of variables (S. and E. Glueck, 1950). The attempt is then made through various methods to find factors that are present in the delinquent sample but absent in the officially nondelinquent control group; the differentiating factors, if found, are said to be "the causal factors" in delinquency. No study to date has located a constellation of biographical factors that significantly distinguish convicted criminals from carefully matched noncriminals. In fact, the history of such investigations has been the successive abandonment of hypotheses that proposed that particular kinds of factors were effective discriminators (Vold, 1958); these hypotheses included the ideas that criminals were biologically inferior, mentally retarded, mentally ill, maternally deprived, economically deprived or a combination of all these plus others.

Implicit and occasionally explicit in the writings of criminologists who follow this tradition and methodology is the idea that if only such differences could be located, namely, "the causes" of crime, society could do something about the treatment or reformation of individual criminals. Similarly, if we knew "the causes," we could begin to develop techniques for the prevention and elimination of crime. The kind of preventive actions or treatment program that would be developed would presumably be dependent on the sorts of factors said to differentiate criminals from noncriminals, but they would have one thing in common: They would all be particularistic in their restriction to a few factors. They would develop programs aimed at "correcting" the particular factors thought to generate delinquency or crime; if individual maladjustment were proposed as "the cause" of delinquency, individual counseling and psychotherapy would be the corollary treatment; if the poor physical and social amenities of the community were seen as the delinquency generating forces, community projects aimed at the improvement of selected facilities would be seen as the answer; if the adolescent peer group were seen as the source of delinquency, perhaps new ways of working with youths would be proposed as ways of lowering delinquency rates. When such preventive and reformative programs have been put into practice and carefully evaluated, they have had no significant effects on community delinquency rates (McCord, 1959; Kobrin, 1959; and Miller, 1962).

The selectivity of treatment or preventive actions is the natural corollary of the highly selective and particularistic explanations of crime causation that have characterized criminology, and the failure of such remedial actions becomes understandable when viewed from the sociological perspective adopted here. Before outlining this alternative perspective, a brief review of the main stumbling blocks in the path of traditional criminological explanations is useful. The traditional assumption that those who commit criminal acts possess traits that differentiate them from noncriminals has produced methodologies that blind criminologists to the processes of *selection* which characterize every stage of law enforcement. The result has been decades of research in which varieties of samples of official offenders have been searched for factors thought to differentiate them from non-rule breakers.

The assumption that criminals are different from non criminals fails to deal with the following problems. In the first place, by limiting its attention to the individuals found guilty by the courts, criminology becomes the study of the failed offender, that is, the offender who was unlucky enough to be caught and convicted. In fact, and even more narrowly, because of easy access for research, criminologists have largely concentrated on the failed offenders who have been placed in institutions. There are two basic problems of sampling here: First, is the convicted criminal population representative of all those committing criminal acts in a society; and second, is a sample of individuals drawn from selected penal institutions representative of all convicted criminals or even of all institutionalized criminals? As the answers to both these questions are negative, it follows that the assertions or generalizations about causation proposed by those who ignore these questions are automatically invalidated. Such questions have either been completely ignored in criminology or they have received lip service only to be ignored in actual research practice.

A second issue related to the problem of sampling concerns those offenders who, although they are discovered by either the law enforcers or others such as employers, are dealt with informally, thereby escaping public identification and the official criminal label. Restriction of sampling and research to the officially convicted criminal thus falls a long way short of the statistically acceptable sampling criteria to which criminologists nominally subscribe.

Clearly what traditional criminology and most earlier sociology completely ignored were the processes by which only some people are selected for official processing. Criminologists begin their work after the complex selecting and sifting processes are completed, and their analyses seem based on the assumption that such processes are a reliable constant—invariant according to time or place. Some feeling for what they were missing can be obtained from Cicourel's (1968) study of the official construction of delinquency rates in two apparently very similar towns. Given their similarity, one would have expected the towns to have provided only marginally different patterns of delinquency, but different forms of police organisation and policies of enforcement between the towns resulted in routine enforcement practices which produced considerable variation in the official definition of and consequent rates of delinquency.

A third barrier in the way of traditional approaches to explanation is encountered in their inability to deal with those forms of behavior that are very similar to officially defined crime in terms of motives and consequences but are almost completely immune from the official detection, trial, and labeling processes. Many occupations, for example, provide opportunities for a wide variety of property offenses (Martin, 1962); employees often claim that systematic distortion of expense accounts or the removal of the organization's stationery for personal use are simply "fringe benefits" that go with the job (Chapman, 1968). However, their occupational immunity means that only the smallest fraction of such offenders ever receive the official criminal label.

Finally, it is worth reemphasizing that a recognition of the cultural and temporal relativity of the definition of crime and the reactions to crime calls into question the entire approach of traditional criminology and its assumptions and thus requires an abandonment of the naive search for universal causes of criminality. By creating new laws outlawing different forms of behavior (for example, in relation to the use of motor vehicles in the twentieth century) and by removing or altering old laws (for example, in relation to abortion) society is constantly redefining what is criminal and at the same time actually *creating* and *eliminating* crime by definition; these continuous processes of redefinition require different approaches to the problems of explanation from those adopted by traditional criminology.

The result of ignoring considerations such as these has meant that criminology has been an adaptive or "normative" discipline. To the extent that it accepts existing official definitions and practices as its defining criteria, it becomes little more than a covert tool of social policy and a conservative force in society. The situation is one in which contemporary criminologists make claims to the objectivity of an empirical science and then abrogate this claim by their willingness to undertake research into such social problems as the change of offenders, the evaluation of treatment methods, or the development of typologies of treatment. When criminologists undertake work of this kind, they move from the role of the impartial scientist and take up that of the political man; for example, in undertaking an investigation into the relative efficacy of imprisonment and probation for certain types of offenders, the criminologist, by his very willingness to carry out the project, is implicitly accepting that prison or probation are in themselves useful or appropriate for certain individuals convicted by the courts.

This charge applies particularly to those investigators who take over the official definitions of the problem and work *within* them, when researchers accept the official aims of the control, punishment, or reformation of individual offenders and attempt to evaluate these their work necessarily rests on an implicit acceptance of both changing the individual as a value in itself and also the value of changing him or her in the particular direction required by the society at that point in time. Such an acceptance is a political act, for it rests on both an agreement with the desirability of changing individuals and a satisfaction with the penal processes that sift out those who eventually receive the official stamp of criminality. In effect, this kind of researcher says; "Those individuals sifted out by the penal system as criminals should be changed in some way, for their own good or for the good of society, and I can help to find the most effective form of change." Acceptance of the need for change, the direction of change, and the criteria for evaluating effectiveness of the processes of change all rest on values that are ultimately political in character; they are political because they reflect beliefs about how the society ought to be run and about the kinds of people society ought to contain.

The questions that must always be asked of such evaluative research is: What are the criteria for determining "effectiveness," and whose interests do they serve? I suggest that criminology has too frequently worked on the basis of implicit assumptions about the need *to do something* to individual offenders, thereby allying itself to controllers or therapists. The alternative strategy proposed here is for the sociologist to suspend commitment to any norm of action in his work and to subject existing practices of control and therapy to sociological analysis. Goffman's (1961) analysis of a mental hospital is a lucid example of sociological description in which commitment to therapeutic values has been suspended and replaced by an attitude of sociological disinterest; the commitment here is to certain forms of reflection and description.

This is not to denigrate this sort of research in itself but rather to demonstrate its spurious claims to certain kinds of objectivity and impartiality; insofar as the criminologist undertaking this kind of research recognizes its implicit prescriptive character and hence his own part in the creation of social and penal policy, the criticism is redundant. In fact, the extent of a society's willingness to undertake this kind of evaluative research may be taken as an index of its acceptance of the value of a limited rationality in social policy. Such an acceptance marks a radical break with traditional approaches to innovation in social policy in which we have acted first and thought afterwards. (These issues are discussed in more detail in the last chapter.)

The problem of responsibility

A final problem that must be raised concerns the concept of legal responsibility. The legal systems of industrial
societies are based on the concept of individual responsibility; after a series of complex legal procedures, accused
individuals are found to be either guilty or not guilty of
acts legally defined as criminal. Embodied in the concept of
the "guilty mind" are the ideas that the individual knew
that what he was doing (or not doing) was against the law
and that he acted with intent. The law itself allows that
responsibility can be lessened by a range of mitigating circumstances (for example, when the victim is found to have
severely provoked the attacker); this may result either in
the individuals being found guilty of a lesser crime, as when
the person charged with murder is found guilty of man-
slaughter or, at the court's discretion, in his simply being
given a less severe sentence. There are, of course, a very
small number of "absolute liability" offenses in which the
concept of the "guilty mind" is redundant.

The proportion of convicted persons who are found to be
mentally abnormal in some way and not therefore responsible in the conventional legal sense is miniscule.
Walker (1965, p. 282) shows that in 1961 they formed 0.65
per cent of all adults found guilty by the courts in England
and Wales; there is a range of special court orders used
for dealing with such cases. Clearly, then, over 99 percent
of convicted adult offenders were found to be legally responsible for their illegal acts.

Because of the absence of data, it is impossible to compare accurately the situation in the United States; however,
in a study of criminal responsibility and mental disability,
Matthews (1970) analyzed the use of the defense of insanity in a sample of large American cities. In general, the
defense of insanity was used very infrequently; for exam-

ple, in California in 1965 out of 36,643 felony dispositions, a plea of not guilty by reason of insanity was entered in only 464 cases (1.3 percent of the total). Out of this number, 195 cases (0.53 percent) were tried in which the plea of insanity had not been withdrawn, and of these, 109 were acquitted. Matthews estimates that roughly three-fifths of the acquittals were on the grounds of insanity. With the exception of Washington, D.C., there was little variation between jurisdictions in the use of the insanity defense; thus, the use of this defense of nonresponsibility through insanity appears to be as infrequent in the United States as in England.

Once the court has established "normal" guilt "beyond all reasonable doubt," it then goes on to punish the convicted offenders, choosing from the range of sentences available to it.

The penal processes involved in deciding on criminal responsibility and attached punishments enshrine beliefs about human behavior that are rarely articulated in our everyday transactions with others; however, such beliefs seem to be so fundamental in our society as to be implicit in much of our social behavior. These beliefs, which are "taken for granted" in most situations (Schuetz, 1967), concern particularly the individual's ability to choose from among a variety of projects of action; thus, in the penal system, in holding an individual to be responsible for the commission of an illegal act, we are saying that he could have chosen otherwise, he could have chosen not to commit the act. The public and ritual nature of legal dramas in our society effectively institutionalizes and constantly reinforces social beliefs about free will and choice. By upholding this belief in the crucial area of illegal behavior, we are granted automatic license to extend it to the rest of our social behavior. For most people, their common-sense understanding of their world includes implicit beliefs about choice and responsibility: A man "chooses" a wife; an adolescent "chooses" when to quit one job and take another; a housewife "chooses" one brand of soap over another. Our common-sense understanding of the world tells us that choice operates at all levels from our most far-reaching to our most trivial decisions.

Unfortunately, this common-sense view of social action is in fundamental contradiction to much research done in criminology and sociology, and a major problem facing sociological explanation is how to reconcile the common-sense view of the world held by the subjects of sociological investigation with the determinism of much of their theorizing and research methods. A primary characteristic of most criminological theory and research has been its acceptance of a naive positivism and views of causation that characterized the natural sciences in earlier stages of their development. The core assumption seems to be that a given criminal act is simply a product of antecedent conditions: The act is determined by the preceding underlying biographical conditions of the criminal. According to this perspective, the criminologist's problem is to locate the pattern of background factors that determined the commission of the criminal act; such factors could be chemical, physical, psychological, or social in character. But this notion of partial determinism conflicts with the concept of legal responsibility and choice; the dilemma is this: If any individual's criminal act is determined by antecedent conditions, how can the individual criminal be held responsible? Taken to its logical conclusion, the determinist position is a denial of the relevance of the legal and punishment process; it states that the individual had no choice but to commit the act in question. This is naive or partial determinism because it does not apply the same logic to the activities of the police, the judge, the lawyers, and the criminological investigator himself; the complete determinist would argue that everybody's acts were determined—the judge's and the criminologist's as much as the criminal's. In this view, society becomes rather like the first rehearsal of a play in which the stage is set, the parts are cast, and the actors stumble more or less haltingly through their predetermined lines. Proponents of this perspective in the human sciences argue that the determinants of behavior exist, that they can be located by getting as close as possible to what they take to be natural scientific methods of investigation and that the aim therefore of such a criminology is the prediction of criminality. By extension, the proponents argue that once we have managed to predict the "who," the "when," and the "where" of criminality, then we will be able to do something about it.

The persistence of the criminological determinists' basic belief that crime in general can be explained by the analysis of convicted offenders' biographies is not as surprising as many initially appear. While the other social sciences have had since their inception ongoing and heated philosophical debates about the appropriate theoretical perspectives and methodological styles to adopt in their analyses of the social world, there has been a complete dearth of this kind of discussion within criminology. The continuous questioning of its philosophical basis and the assumptions on which it rests, which has characterized sociology, is completely absent from criminology, and one can look in vain through the academic criminological journals for any fundamental debate about the assumptions on which it rests. This absence of philosophical debate within criminology has contributed considerably to the persistence of naive assumptions about causation and prevention; the absence of self-questioning also reinforces the view that criminology, in claiming scientific status, is laying a thin veneer of academic respectability over its implicit ideology.

A further point about responsibility, will, and choice is worth making as an introduction to the alternative perspective. Not only do certain ideas about responsibility (which differ radically from positivist conceptions of it) underpin the alternative to be proposed, but the latter also recommends that we treat "responsibility" as an empirical phenomenon—as an "event in the world"—and hence worthy of investigation in itself. We can observe that within the penal system different conceptions of responsibility are held at different stages of the penal process by the different occupational groups who work the system and in relation to different kinds of offenders(see Duster, 1969; Stoll, 1968; Aubert and Messinger, 1958). These differing conceptions of responsibility (how blame is apportioned and its consequences) will be constituent features of, for example, the occupational ideologies of different groups of officials. Policemen, judges, prison officers, probation officers, social workers, officially designated offenders, and others are likely to differ considerably in the "model of man" they tacitly employ in their everyday work. Thus, among other things, they are likely to see the "causes" of an offense, the societal reaction appropriate for an offender, and the offender's future (his corrigibility) in quite different terms. It is through these differences that the offender's official biography is socially constructed.

Conclusion

The way the positivist perspective has been applied in criminology and the results of its application suggest that it is based on mistaken and limiting assumptions about social behavior in general and criminal behavior in particular. The alternative perspective adopted here is based on different assumptions, has different aims, has different methods, and has a different subject matter to those of traditional criminology. The approach is, on the one hand, more encompassing in that it moves away from the narrow focus on the individual convicted criminal to the broader issues of situations, social processes, and social structures and, on the other hand, less imperialistic in its rejection of the search for universal causes of crime with its implicit prescriptions for treatment and prevention. The broad outlines of this alternative are presented in the next chapter.

2

An Alternative Perspective

Introduction

If sociology is to improve on traditional criminological orientations it must come to terms with the stumbling blocks that impeded the development of criminology. While I recognize that such a perspective will inevitably face different analytical problems of its own, my suggestion here is that they do not have the inherently intractable character of those faced by traditional perspectives. Core problems to be overcome include the scope and level of analysis, the related problem of the normative character of criminology, and the production of forms of sociological research and description that make man the *subject* and not the object of study; in other words, in its rejection of positivisms it recognizes the human character of social action. The import of this emphasis on the subject will be elaborated shortly. No attempt is made here to provide an all-embracing theory of crime and delinquency; rather, a perspective is presented that directs the sociological observer to certain kinds of analytic problems and questions, and at the same time, bypasses the criminological stumbling blocks. Some general features of this perspective are outlined before its solutions for the traditional problems are spelled out.

The concepts of deviance and conformity

The proposed alternative places the study of crime and delinquency within the broader and more inclusive sociological analysis of social deviance. Following Cohen (1966), social deviance can be defined, for the moment, simply as behavior that violates normative rules; normative rules refer to those guides for behavior that orient an individual's actions in any interaction with others. These normative rules and expectations can range from the "taken-for-granted" implicit guides that go unquestioned by the actor in his everyday activities, such as the rule that directs men in our society to wear trousers, through the more formal rules for action that operate in work, educational, and other formal organizations, to the most explicit and formal set of rules embodied in the criminal and other kinds of law. In sociology the concept of rule has a wider meaning than in our everyday use of the word; in everyday usage we tend to think of a rule as an explicit formal statement that tells us what we should or should not do in given situations. The rules of organized games epitomize our everyday usage of the term: The "rules of the game" are agreed in principle by all the participants before the game commences, and the mutual agreements to abide by them furnish the conditions that allow the game to begin and proceed. Similarly, at school or at work there are usually formal, precise statements that are attempts to furnish the conditions for orderly interaction by stating the boundaries of acceptable conduct. However, the sociologist extends the everyday meaning of the term *rule* to include those guides for behavior that may be relatively informal, implicit, and frequently unstated in the course of our interaction with each other. By including in the term *rule,* the complete range of guides for behavior, from the most formal to the most informal, from those operative in an individual's most trivial to those in his most important decisions, the sociologist is making his task very complex. Although it may seem an apparently simple task to define the most formal rules and their conditions of applicability, at the other end of the continuum the definition of the implicit and informal rules may be an extremely complicated exercise.

One of the basic assumptions that informs sociological investigation is that there are rules or norms that serve as guides for the action of the participant in all situations of social interaction. It follows that a primary task of sociology is to analyze the content and the various qualities of these rules or norms. In particular, the sociologist would want to describe the conditions of applicability of any given rule, especially the range and types of situations in which it was applicable and the range of social statuses and roles that were subject to it. The flexibility of the rule would be important too—that is, how far individuals were free to modify it or to implement their own verbal or behavioral interpretation of it. A thorough analysis would also require a study of the history of the rule: How did it emerge, who created it and whose interests did it represent initially? Does it still represent the same interests or have these changed? A necessary corollary of these questions about the derivation and qualities of the rule would be the study of reactions to deviations from it; this would entail asking a range of questions about how the rule is maintained or enforced. The kinds of sanctions used to deal with those who deviate from the rule, from physical violence to mild social disapproval, and their effects would similarly be a central concern of this approach.

These considerations mean, in effect, that the study of social deviance becomes, as Cohen points out, the study of deviance, conformity, and control. Deviance can only be understood effectively within this more inclusive perspective which relates questions about deviation to questions about conformity, with particular emphasis being placed on the forms of social control mediating between deviation and conformity. This perspective views the amount and quality of deviance in a society or any part of a society as the product of the interaction between deviants and potential deviants, and the society's or group's social control mechanisms. It is therefore necessary to look at both sides of the coin to understand deviance—that is, at those who deviate and in what situations and at those who attempt to enforce the rule and with what techniques and effects.

Implicit in this approach is the view that an understanding of conformity—that is, of the "normal" or the "non-deviant"—is an essential complement to an understanding of the "abnormal" or deviant. The question is asked: Can we really understand the abnormal unless we thoroughly understand the normal at the same time? Posing this question draws attention to a further failing of traditional criminology; all too frequently criminologists and sociologists made assumptions about what they considered to be the "normal" or the "noncriminal" and prejudged the abnormality of the criminal. The assumption was made that "normal" people did not break the law and that therefore those who did must be "abnormal;" their law-breaking was viewed as a symptom of some inner abnormality or pathology.

The investigators' assumptions about what was normal rested typically on their own personal, usually middle-class, values; behaviors that deviated radically from the investigator's strongly held but implicit personal values were diagnosed as abnormal, and the roots of the abnormalities were sought either in physical or psychological pathologies. A failure to spell out the dimensions of normality and their distribution in society meant that assertions about the abnormality of offenders by criminologists rested on their common-sense assumptions about the rightness and wrongness of some behaviors. Diagnosis of abnormality thus frequently coincided conveniently with strongly held moral beliefs, so that behaviors felt to be morally wrong from one ethical standpoint were consequently also diagnosed as pathological. This resulted in much tautologous argument in which the convicted criminal was defined as "abnormal" or "pathological" because of his criminality, and then this assumed "abnormality" was used to explain his criminality. So unless the investigator carefully defines what he means by "normal" and actually shows how it is distributed within society or a social group, then many of his assertions about the "abnormal" or the "deviant" may be based on entirely false assumptions about the normal dimensions of the behaviors he is investigating. An essential prerequisite of any analysis of deviance in relation to a given rule or norm would seem to be the clear and precise definitions of the non-deviant together with some attempt to show its empirical distribution in society, rather than the traditional reliance on assumptions about the distribution of normality.

According to this perspective, then, criminal and delinquent behaviors become particular examples of the general phenomenon of social deviance. The processes involved in deviation from specifically legal norms can be compared to the processes resulting in other forms of deviance; the sociologist argues that analysis of the similarities and differences in the processes of deviance from substantively different norms should enhance sociological understanding more than the study of any given form of deviance in isolation. This perspective opens up an enormous range of subject matter for the student of social deviance. Not only does it include many of the behaviors traditionally designated as social problems by society, such as crime, mental illness, narcotic addiction, and alcoholism, it also includes areas not so designated. For example, certain kinds of unconventional or innovative behaviors can be viewed from a social deviance perspective. Thus, social groups concerned with modifying or breaking accepted canons of practice in any sphere, from the artistic to the political, can be seen as deviant; many occupational groups in our society are granted license to deviate from accepted styles and practices in their occupation: Artists of all kinds, fashion designers and certain kinds of scientists all have license to innovate stylistically and change accepted practices.

Very often this license to innovate stylistically, which is granted both by other artists, their typical "reference group," and by large sections of the public, is accompanied by a more general expectation that artists will also be unconventional in their behavior; when they meet these expectations their flouting of conventions is generally tolerated. The social tolerance accorded to artists' stylistic and behavioral deviations contrasts with the lack of tolerance shown to other deviant groups.

In the fields of religious or political behavior, there are groups whose ideologies, beliefs and behaviors are sufficiently different from the conventional political and religious approaches of a society to render them deviant. Moreover, this kind of deviance may not be so remote from criminal deviance as it might initially appear; it may be that different forms of deviance emerge in the same parts of society and that any individual might as easily become a political or religious deviant as a criminal or narcotic addict. This kind of consideration might be relevant in any analysis of deviance in some of the black ghettoes of the large American cities where a range of extreme political and religious sects flourish alongside narcotic and criminal subgroups. Taken to its logical conclusion, this approach proposes that deviance can be studied in any situation where social norms exist as guides for action; wherever there is a social group, deviation from its norms can be studied, whether the norms are formal and precise or im-

plicit and ambiguous. However, as will be suggested subsequently, a more circumscribed and limited use of the
concept of deviance may help to increase its clarity.

The scope and level of analysis

Apart from the difficulties peculiar to this perspective,
can such an approach come to terms with the problems
faced by traditional criminology? Let us take the scope and
level of analysis first. The limitation of criminology to a
focus on the convicted criminal meant that its explanations
of crime and criminality rested on hypotheses and research
relating to the convicted criminal population alone. Further, in terms of aim, the kinds of explanation proposed,
although claiming to explain crime and criminality in general, in practice offered explanations of individual criminality—that is, what caused any given individual to commit
criminal acts. The social deviance perspective on crime
differs radically both in focus and in aim; convicted criminals become only one particular group of legal norm
breakers whose processing by the penal system may have
important implications for their subsequent criminality.
The main focus would be on the processes of creating, maintaining, enforcing, and breaking of legal and allied norms;
these processes are understandable only by their placement
in a societal context. The aim would not be the explanation
of individual criminality in terms of a group of individual
biographical factors, but rather an understanding of the
social nature of crime as the constantly changing product
of a wide variety of complex social processes. An integral
part of this aim would be to demonstrate how the quantity
and quality of crime in a given society is related to the
prevailing conditions of life at the time of analysis. In other
words, crime is to be understood by showing how it is bound
up with the noncriminal features of a society. To take crime

out of its social context and to try to explain it as the product of a minority of unfortunate individuals apparently
"outside" the boundaries of conventional society has been
a cardinal sin of traditional criminology.

The "value" problem

The perspective also comes to terms much more satisfactorily with the value problems involved in the scientific
analysis of crime than does traditional criminology which,
as we saw in Chapter I, is a normative discipline. An unquestioned acceptance of the legal status quo, with the
related refusal to ask certain kinds of questions and the
willingness of criminologists to involve themselves practically in evaluating or recommending reformative, preventive, treatment, and punitive penal programs epitomize the
normative character of criminology; they are the "value"
problems that contradict criminologists' claims to objectivity. The alternative perspective has as its fundamental
aim the improvement of sociological understanding and not
"the solution" to the social problem of crime and delinquency. The key distinction in approach would be that the
investigation of norms and deviance from them would be
empirical—that is, it would attempt to describe and display
the ways in which social action is rule guided; the criteria
of normality would be the criteria used and displayed by
members themselves rather than the observers' assumptions about what was normal. What the sociologist tries to
describe and understand are the many characteristics of
the norms that actually orient people's conduct in their
interaction with others; this necessitates focusing on the
meanings individuals give to the multitude of situations
faced in everyday life and describing the patterns these
social meanings form. By describing these patterns of social
meanings that guide behavior and are created, maintained,

and modified by the actors themselves and by showing the
methods for their production, the sociologist can prevent
the intrusion of his own assumptions and values to a much
greater extent than was possible within the limited and
normative focus of traditional criminology.

The study of norms in use

In this perspective, legal norms are simply seen as one
group of norms among many; they are abstract and formal
and may enter any individual's consciousness only rarely
as actual guides for action. The social deviance approach
proposes that the sociological understanding of the distribution of the violations of legal norms in society and the
complementary distribution of reactions to such violations
can only be derived from a knowledge of the actual norms
that orient people's behavior. Fortunately, this daunting
task is partially simplified by the remarkable consistency
that characterizes patterns of social interaction. An illustration of the implications of such an approach can be given
by the following example. The traditional assumption that
property offenses are almost entirely confined to the lower
working class is quickly called into question when middle-
class behavior is actually examined; thus many property
offenses are viewed simply as occupational perquisites,
and this is reinforced by their immunity from law enforcement. In this case, functionally equivalent behavior—
removing property that does not belong to you—is given
different social meanings both by those undertaking the
behavior and those responsible for enforcement (Chapman, 1968). A major sociological task is to analyze the
norms that actually orient actions in everyday situations
and to examine the social processes through which these
different social meanings emerge and are maintained.

In the non-normative approach then, the sociologist takes

the actor's own definitions and meanings as his data and does not allow his own value assumptions about, for example, the necessity for law and order, to guide or limit his data selection. This is a simplified description of the non-normative approach, and it raises many theoretical and methodological issues that are central to sociology in general (some of these will be elaborated in subsequent discussion).

The treatment of responsibility in sociological interpretation

The final problem with which an alternative perspective has to come to terms is the issue of individual responsibility. The dilemma to be faced is the irreconcilability of the legal and everyday common-sense models of behavior with the deterministic scientific models employed in traditional criminological analysis. Models of the former generally see the individual as possessing, within certain limits, choice or free will, although deterministic scientific models propose that the phenomenon to be explained (such as a criminal act) is "caused" or "determined" by antecedent conditions. The ultimate implication of the deterministic model is to deny the legitimacy and relevance of legal and common-sense models of man. If everything is determined, the idea of choice becomes superfluous. Traditional criminology was particularly characterized by deterministic theories and methods; its styles of theorizing and investigation rested on the same sorts of assumptions as those upon which the natural sciences rest in their explanation of natural phenomena.

In fact, much sociology has also been and still is characterized by these deterministic approaches to explanation, and the debate continues about the most appropriate perspective for the sociologist to adopt towards his subject matter (Winter, 1966). Briefly, the debate is between two broad groups. There are those who claim that social phenomena and natural phenomena are very similar, that therefore the application of scientific methods and assumptions to social phenomena is appropriate, and that eventually sociologists will be able to formulate laws about social behavior in the same way natural scientists derive laws. The other side is represented by those who argue that social phenomena are fundamentally different from natural phenomena and that therefore the kinds of statements that can be made about social phenomena will be unlike the laws of natural science. This assertion of the fundamental difference between social and natural phenomena stems from the fact that the objects of the natural world have no inherent meaning, whereas social phenomena only exist through their meanings. Similarly, protagonists of this viewpoint would suggest that natural scientific methods and assumptions have only a limited usefulness in sociology because they can only tell part of the story and other methods are needed to complement them. A central difference of the two approaches is found in the stance of the observer toward the social phenomena being studied. The theories and methods of the deterministic criminologist view man as an object whose actions are determined by internal and external forces, whereas the sociologist working in the interpretive tradition (which was first formulated coherently by Max Weber [1948]) sees man as first and foremost a *choosing* subject; this tradition, complemented by the symbolic interactionism of George Herbert Mead (1934), has been developed, elaborated, and revised by Alfred Schuetz (1967). New directions and impetuses are given to the tradition in the ethnomethodology of Harold Garfinkel (1967). The interpretive sociologist's analytical problem is to describe and reveal how members' everyday procedures and activities routinely produce and sustain a social world; it is these methodic procedures that are glossed in sociologists' conventional reliance on concepts such as "social structure," "status," or "role."

The aims of the alternative perspective

One distinction between the two approaches that is relevant to the analysis of crime concerns their goals. One goal of natural scientific investigation is to locate *the* cause or the *causes* of phenomena, while the goal of the other perspective is not "the causes" but rather certain kinds of "understanding" or interpretation of social phenomena. This understanding is qualitatively rather different from causal explanation; essentially it seeks to understand the processes by which actors arrive at their particular pattern of choices and to describe the actors' perceptions of the limits of these choices. The methodological procedures through which such an understanding can be obtained are rather different from the classical scientific method; these differences should emerge more clearly in the subsequent discussion of actual research projects and theories concerned with crime and delinquency. For the sake of brevity the two approaches will be referred to as the positivist (natural scientific) and interpretive (humanistic) approaches to explanation; traditional criminology epitomizes the positivist approach, while the proposed alternative adopts the interpretive model.

A basic implication of adopting the interpretive approach is the abandonment of the search for the universal cause or causes of crime and a recognition that crime can only be understood through a knowledge of the particular social structure and social processes within and through which it occurs. The cultural and temporal relativity of such understanding contradicts the search for universal causes.

In the light of these two approaches, how can the issue of individual responsibility be dealt with? The suggestion here is that the most effective explanation is one that comes to terms with common-sense understandings and beliefs about choice and especially with the fact that most people in most situations see themselves as possessing a range of choices of action. That the implicit assumptions of the positivist approach, by denying that the actor can choose between projects of action, are out of line with legal and common-sense understandings of action, suggests that the interpretive approach is more appropriate for the understanding of social phenomena.

The focus on members' own accounts

Two further justifications are proposed in support of the interpretive approach. First, by adopting this approach, attention is drawn to something that has been largely ignored by criminology but is given a certain importance in our legal processing of criminals and is accorded importance in everyday explanations of criminal or any other behavior. This is the actor's motivation. From an interpretive perspective, motivation is a central focus of analysis, for the sociologist argues that motives are socially learned and are differentially distributed in the social structure (Gerth and Mills, 1961); his interest centers on the shared patterns of motivation, their meanings for a social group, and the ways they are expressed in action. Much importance is thus given to the social meanings actors give to their own and others' behavior and to the situations they experience. An individual's explanations of his past activities and his future intentions constitute for him the "why" of his behavior or his motivations, and it is these that become some of the most important raw material for the interpretive sociologist. However, the sociologist's main concern is with the *social* character of motivation rather than with each individual's unique pattern of motives; his interest is in the shared motives, in the socially typical rather than the uniquely personal. Thus an analysis of the social distribution of patterns of motivation—how motives emerge, are learned, and transmitted—becomes central in this perspective; the sociologist tries to understand men's actions, in part, by examining the social bases of their motivation, and their methods for making their actions socially intelligible.

This differs from traditional criminology in a fundamental way. Members' own accounts were rarely seen as relevant in explaining crime and delinquency; they were simply by-products of preceding forces. According to the positivist perspective, these preceding forces determined motivation so that a study of actors' motivations was superfluous; what was important was to locate these preceding underlying forces. Values, attitudes, and beliefs, of central importance to the interpretive sociologist and closely bound up with patterns of motivation, were largely disregarded by criminologists in explanations of criminality. On the rare occasions when they were considered—for example, in psychoanalytic explanations (Friedlander, 1947; Glover, 1960)—they were viewed largely as a means of getting at the "real" underlying explanatory factors in the criminal's life experience and as expressions of the actor's unconscious wishes. In other words, the actor's own accounts and his stated values and motivations were hardly ever taken at their face value as meaningful and important data in themselves. The use the sociologist makes of such accounts will depend particularly on the kind of relationship he had with the respondent, the sort of situation in which he obtained the material and the nature of the material sought.

The fact that this emphasis on patterns of stated values and motivations is in line with our everyday commonsense and our legal explanations of conduct is directly re-

lated to the second justification for the interpretive perspective. If the sociologist uses the same sort of data in his
explanations and interpretations of events as other members of the society use in their interpretations, it ought to
facilitate his task of making his explanations meaningful to
the members of that society. The social scientist's problem
of communicating his explanations and interpretations of
events and processes is important for practical reasons.
First, the sociologist is frequently employed directly by
somebody seeking answers to or data about what, for him,
is a problem; thus, after completing his research, the sociologist has the task of making his findings meaningful to his
sponsor. Second, at a more abstract level, the entire relevance of sociology to its social context can be called into
question if its models of explanation cannot be translated
into terms that make sense to the vast majority of nonsociologists in the society; if it is difficult or impossible to trans-
late sociological interpretations into terms that make sense
to members of the surrounding society, it would seem to
call into question the viability of the discipline. For example, it could be suggested that extreme forms of behavior-
istic psychology, in which extrapolations are made from
animal behavior and applied to human behavior, have already reached the situation of alienation from everyday
explanations of conduct in society.

Thus the kinds of models of man with which sociology
operates could be relevant to the meaning people give to
sociology in a society. If it operates with models of man that
are very different from the common-sense models by
which people operate, it will be seen as largely irrelevant,
and the problems of communication between sociologists
and nonsociologists will be acute; yet the closer the congruence of sociological and everyday common-sense models,
the easier are the problems of communication and the more
relevant are the sociological interpretations to the members

of the society. The explanation or understanding of crime and delinquency provides a good example of this problem, for it is in this very field that our society continually upholds and reinforces common-sense beliefs about choice and individual responsibility; thus for the sociologist or criminologist to offer explanations of crime that are based on opposing deterministic models of man would be to directly contradict a very basic common-sense assumption which underpins our social structure.

While the interpretive model can be seen as reflecting the model of man that courts employ practically in deciding on guilt or innocence, it is worth noting that the legal model may change dramatically *after* a finding of guilt. In disposing of or dealing with convicted offenders, courts and penal institutions may quickly discard the "responsibility" model and move toward the adoption of more deterministic models. In punitive or reformative therapy, the underlying model may posit man as effectively constrained by external conditions or driven by internal forces beyond his conscious control. Rather than picturing man as deciding on or determining his own course of action, he is seen as over-determined by a variety of conditions.

The interpretive approach, therefore, directs the sociologist's attention to what people actually think and feel about their own and others' actions and is based upon assumptions about man that are relatively in tune with the common-sense assumptions of the members of the society. What kinds of interpretations are offered that purport to take account of our assumptions about individual responsibility and choice?

Levels of interpretation

The interpretive approach does not look for *the* cause or the *causes* of crime but offers certain kinds of under-

standing and interpretations of crime and delinquency by
placing them in the wider context of social deviance. The
interpretive sociologist would argue that there is a range
of levels of understanding and that the most satisfactory
solution to the problem of explanation occurs when an interpretation considers each level and shows the logical
continuity of understanding between each level; an adequate understanding would rest on the provision of data at
each level and an interpretation that made sense of these
data by showing the links between levels. The particular
level of abstraction and explanation dictates the phenomena to be focussed on and the kinds of questions to be
asked; in turn, the terms of the questions provide for the
kinds of answers to be given. Many of the sociologists who
have proposed theories of crime or delinquency have passed
over or have made assumptions about one or another level
of understanding. They have concentrated on the study of
one level in both their theorizing and their collection of
data, at the same time making explicit or implicit assumptions about the other levels that would fit in with their
interpretation and their data. What are these levels of
understanding that must be integrated for a satisfactory
understanding? Such analytical divisions tend to be arbitrary, but as an illustration, three levels are distinguished
here to demonstrate the explanatory problems involved.

The first level at which it is possible to make statements
about crime and delinquency is that of the total society
being studied, say, the United States or England and Wales.
This is the most abstract level of understanding because
the kinds of statements made at this level are the most remote from the concrete activities of any individual or group;
broad generalizations can be made about apparent trends
in crime, but the kind of generalization or interpretation
proposed will tend to depend on the particular theoretical
stance taken by the observer and hence upon the assump-

tions he makes about the other levels of understanding. Not only do we have the law (which is said to apply to all members of society equally) as a "given" at the level of the total society, but industrial societies also publish a mass of official statistics relating to crime, the activities of the police and the courts, and the penal system; at the same time the official bookkeepers are producing a mass of other official statistics relating to almost every aspect of our lives from income and expenditure to mortality patterns. Given this welter of data, one set of statistics can be correlated with another to see whether changes and trends are random or statistically intercorrelated; the compilation and correlation of a multitude of indexes relating to most aspects of our social life is, with the aid of the computer, a straightforward task, and social scientists frequently use such official statistics to bulwark their interpretations of social events.

However, there are two kinds of assumptions made in using such statistics on their own in an explanation of crime or any other activity. First, the assumption has to be made that the statistics are actually measuring what they claim to be measuring; in other words, can we "trust" the official organizations and take the statistics at their face value? This question raises the sociological problem of the reliability and validity of official data. Second, a set of assumptions has to be made about the actors who have been so neatly summed up in the official statistics; in particular, assumptions have to be made about the kind of people they were, the situations they faced, and their motivations. This type of assumption rests upon models or theories of what man is like, and, as we have seen, there is considerable disagreement among social scientists about this fundamental issue. Both sets of assumptions, then, are statements of the investigator's faith, unless they are supported by empirical data; such data can only be acquired by analysis at the other levels of understanding. Even here, empirical support can only go so far, for no "data" can ground the founding onto-logical and epistemological assumptions present in any in-quiry about the world. Thus, although interpretations that are offered at one level of analysis, may be consistent with the data available at that level, they may not be congruent with data and interpretations at other levels.

For example, a problem of contemporary criminology has been to explain the continuing rise in officially reported property offenses in a period of increasing affluence. Simple economic explanations, which viewed poverty as the main motivating force of such crime, have been replaced by more complex theories like that of Merton (1963), which explains such deviance as a response to the size of the disparity in different parts of society between the goals people strive to achieve (particularly material success) and the actual means provided for their achievement. How-ever, this theory at the level of the total society rests on certain assumptions about individual behavior with which many sociologists would disagree. While Merton's theory may fit the official facts at the societal level, at the experi-ential level of the acting delinquent or criminal its basic assumptions may be largely unfounded.

A second level of analysis might be that of the local com-munity or neighborhood. Many of the prescriptions for so-cial action in relation to delinquency, which may have arisen out of such sociological research into urban delin-quency patterns as that of social ecologists like Shaw and McKay (1942), are based on explanations of delinquency at the level of the local community. They often seem to view the community as something quite autonomous and sep-arate from the wider society, generating delinquency through its own internal social forces. Thus, high rates of delinquency in one area can be explained in terms of the particular characteristics of that community, such as inadequate play facilities, poor housing, or insufficient involvement and participation of members of the community in their own government. The assumption seems to be that the social processes flowing from such features are peculiar to that community and need not be related to its position in the wider social structure. Such a view of the local community may have been more appropriate to the rural communities of preindustrial societies but is somewhat divorced from the social realities of the mass society in which the inhabitants of any subcommunity have a series of complex interrelationships with the central government and other communities. The penetration of any community by other communities and by the formal institutions of the total society is a taken-for-granted part of the world of the man in mass society. Any interpretation of delinquency and crime primarily at the level of the local community should be concerned mainly with the ways in which the particular community is both typical of all such communities in that society and also an integral part of the wider social structure and only secondarily with its unique features.

Finally, explanations at the individual or face-to-face level can all too easily omit a consideration of the forms of the relationships and processes that bind an individual to the surrounding community and to the total society. These omissions characterize much of the writing and research into crime and delinquency that might be labeled as social psychology; the main emphasis is placed on the study of the direct social pressures an individual experiences in his face-to-face relationships with a variety of others. In the field of delinquency, for example, a study of the more important face-to-face relationships might compare the relative importance of family and peer group values to the adolescent and the relationship of such values to delinquent behavior patterns. The individual is seen as being at the intersection of a range of sometimes conflicting and sometimes congruent immediate social pressures to conform to particular values and norms. However, a sociologically meaningful interpretation of delinquency would have to relate such data to the other levels of analysis; on their own they form only a small part of the total picture. Thus, the complex relationships between the individual, the community and the total society must be described and placed within a cohesive framework if an adequate interpretation of crime and delinquency is to be offered. Even when this is done, the grounds for deciding on the adequacy of an interpretation are derived from the set of assumptions and methods that generated the theory in the first place; there are no criteria independent of a particular theoretical standpoint that enable us to choose between theories. Choice of a perspective and its associated set of assumptions for viewing any social phenomenon is ultimately a display of personal commitment. A sociologist's election to work within one theoretical framework rather than another is a display of his personal commitment to the relative importance he gives to some problems over and against others and of his view of sociology and the world. Having made such a choice, his willingness to continue working within the selected perspective will also be related to the ability of the perspective's methodologies to answer convincingly the questions it poses on its own terms. One possible reason for the abandonment of positivism by some sociologists is precisely its failure to locate those differences between "criminal" and "noncriminal" populations that its basic tenets assert.

The relevance of language, meaning, and the socially typical

From the viewpoint of the interpretive sociologist, the central problems are those of trying to reveal members' methodic procedures for producing and sustaining an intelligible social world and of displaying their choice patterns as emergent products of those procedures. Thus, study of the processes of emergence, transmission, maintenance, and modification of social meanings lies at the center of his approach. He chooses to view the social structures as always shifting complexes of social meanings routinely produced and sustained through rule-guided practices. In this context, *social meanings* refer to the shared symbols individuals use to understand and describe the situations they experience. Language is the uniquely human means for the expression of these activities, and it is language that makes the worlds and experiences of others symbolically available for us. It is through language that an individual expresses his intentions, explanations of past actions, the meanings constituting his experiences and relationships, and in general makes himself accountable and intelligible for himself and others. Language, viewed as the means for making social worlds available, is given profound significance by sociologists in the interpretive tradition. Language, as both the means for constituting and at the same time reflectively interpreting and describing the social worlds, becomes a focus of study in itself. A paradox, or obdurate feature of the world that produces complex problems for the sociological observer is that language becomes both the "object" of and the means to analysis. The sociologist must always pay the most careful attention to his own use of language and the claims he makes for his descriptions. There is a strong exhortation to the observer in interpretive sociology to make his own reliance on language for describing the social world as much a critical issue as the language of those he studies; this critical self-awareness should lead to an authentic reflexive sociology that attempts to clarify its own production.

This is not to say that the sociologist reifies language in

making it an object of study; he does not view it as an object that has some kind of independent effect on the outcome of a course of action, but his focus on language is rather on its role as the prime carrier of cultural meanings and man's foremost mode of self-expression. Recent sociology displays how a focus on the social "work" language performs for members can clarify the basic structures of social interaction (see for example, Sudnow 1972; Cicourel, 1964).

In analyzing the linguistically expressed meanings that constitute members' publicly observable choice patterns, the sociologist is concerned not with the individually unique but with the socially typical; shared and common meanings provide for the production of socially recognizable (as "in accord with a rule") and typical actions. A sociological interest, therefore, is in the differential distribution of meanings between groups, for this comprises what sociologists call the "social structure." As this meaningful production is a *process*, an emerging, and an unfolding, the concept of social structure is a gloss for (a term that covers over) the activities that inexorably constitute this unfolding (for the founding discussion of members' glossing practices see, Garfinkel and Sacks, 1970). Social organization comprises typical responses to typical situations; these typical responses arise out of the socially shared or intersubjective processes of interpretation and meaning construction. Perhaps the word *typical* should be qualified in case it gives too static a picture of social relationships. *Typical* means those aspects of attitudes, beliefs, and actions that are shared with others; thus, in relation to any cultural item studied, the sociologist accepts that every individual has his unique perspective, experiences, and interpretations. That is, his interest is in how men together produce a social world.

For example, do the boys who occasionally go on shoplifting expeditions together, in spite of the differences in their individual responses of fear, detachment, or excitement, share common interpretations of the events? Do they typically give the same kind of explanation for their activities? Do their explanations vary depending on to whom they are explaining the events, so that their typical explanations to their friends differ from their typical explanations to their parents, which in turn differ from their typical explanations to juvenile court judges or inquisitive sociologists? Posing this kind of question suggests that any event can have several "typical" meanings and that such meanings will depend very much on the context and relationship in which the account is given. A sociological interest focuses on the production of accounts and how they are both bound to and constitutive of the social context of their production (for useful discussion of the nature of accounts and their relevance to sociology, see Scott and Lyman; 1968, and Harré and Secord, 1972). A good example of the context-bound character of subjects' accounts and the different "fronts" they put up is given by Carol Warren (1972) in describing her study of the homosexual community. Two members she interviewed had very different kinds of involvement with this community, but in observing them with other community members she noted how *both* presented a front suitable for interaction within the community:

> For all intents and purposes the fronts projected to the community at large and to the clique members were *very much the same* for both Ted and Dave. However, the fronts projected to me, the interviewer, were *extremely different.*

The sociologist's comprehension of any kind of event thus depends partly on his ability to obtain these different accounts and to examine their methods of production. Significant contexts for the production of accounts in the sphere of deviance are those situations in which an individual is required to account for his actions or character. Law courts, psychiatric clinics, tribunals, and school principals' offices are obvious examples of places where accounting for oneself is a required but routinized accomplishment.

Choice and the study of the socially typical

How, then, does this style of analysis cope with the problem of choice? Acknowledging man's freedom as a basic ontological premise, this method of sociological reflection tries to display how man's fundamental openness to a world becomes partially closed through his use of routine, taken-for-granted, and socially recognized procedures that constitute the social world. This partial closure, this constitution of the situation as a certain form, shape, and social space, is always seen as an ongoing accomplishment of members. Choice is a situated accomplishment of members, the very choices themselves constituting the situations observed and described by sociologists. Sociological analysis of the production of a meaningful social world and of the differential distribution of typical substantive meanings (such as the typical recipes for handling interaction with the police among different social, ethnic, or age groups) provides ways of understanding how groups symbolically constitute their social action. What emerges from this kind of analysis is that, for any typical situation, there is a picture of typical courses of action, placed against a backdrop of a limited number of perceived alternatives; the individual's choice in any situation arises from these perceived alternatives (see, for example, Bittner, 1967).

Most important, in terms of the question of determinism, the interpretive sociologist argues that any actual choice is situationally contingent and both emerges from and constitutes the individual's stream of consciousness. As another's stream of consciousness is not available for us either as partners to the interaction or as sociological observers, the other's choice becomes socially recognizable and observable only through *our own* interpretive work. This interpretive work is always retrospective (it looks *back* on the completed act, gesture, sentence, or word) and in this backward glance the act can have the *illusion* of determinism—that is, it can be read as *necessarily* produced by its antecedent conditions. This illusion of determinism is partially caught in accounts such as, "It was inevitable under the circumstances," "What else could I do?" "I had no option but to . . . ," Given this view of the contingency of choice and action, the sociologist (as well as any member practically involved in a situation) makes sense of *particular* actions by placing them in the context of the socially typical or routine.

There are two distinct problems here. First, there is the question of innovation and how new responses emerge either to the same or to new situations. In some senses the question of choice seems to be much more important here because the typical responses to new situations do not yet exist and there are usually no clear guides for action or expectations of behavior; thus, understanding the way in which the alternatives are perceived is crucial for the analysis of innovative acts and the emergence of fresh styles of action. Second, there is the maintenance of typical responses to typical situations; here responses or solutions to the typical situations have already been worked out and are frequently well established or institutionalized. They are given to the newcomer as the accepted ways of dealing with the situation. In this case the form of the perceived alternatives will be different from that of the first situation; acceptance of the existing typical responses will depend not so much on the process of weighing up and reflecting on the perceived alternatives but rather on what the individual takes for granted in his social world, on the things he never questions. Both these problems are relevant to particular theories of delinquency that attempt to deal with the emergence and maintenance of what various writers have referred to as the delinquent subculture.

The view of choice the sociologist adopts, then, is inevitably a compromise between fully blown determinism and a state of completely open consciousness.

An early move to reorient sociological analysis of crime and delinquency towards some of these issues was made by David Matza (1964); he characterizes his position as 'soft determinism.' Matza's discussion of choice (modified in a later work (1969), is strongly antithetical to the traditional positivisms of criminology and sociology; it has clear affinities with the legal model of choice that can be viewed as a highly articulated version of members' routine, taken-for-granted ways of understanding choice in their everyday activities. Matza thus goes some way towards introducing common-sense understandings of responsibility and choice into sociological rhetoric. However, while Matza's interest is in recommending a view of responsibility as a *criterion* for doing good or adequate sociological description, my recommendation is to treat members' routine decisions about responsibility and choice as methods for deciding the character of events. That is to say, rather than trying to describe what choice and responsibility "really are," the sociological task would be to describe the methods for their routine accomplishment; Matza's description would then be one among several competing methods for allocating responsibility (as indeed also would be my own preceding discussion). However, as it is a method that in its elaborated form relies on a sophisticated reading of sociology and philosophy, it is not likely to be a method commonly practiced by members.

One way of viewing choice within an interpretive framework is to analyze the typical kinds of limitations that provide the horizons within which choice operates; these would include both consciously perceived limitations and the unquestioned framework within which such limitations are brought to consciousness. The limitations or restrictions on behavior are almost always social rather than physical; only in extreme situations, such as contact with society's formal agents of social control such as the police or prison officers, is the choice of adults limited by physical pressures. The source of such social pressures is always other people, yet crucially, these pressures are not external to us in any way (except in the limiting case of physical force), for they are composed of our internal symbolic constructions of such pressures. They comprise, in particular, the ways in which we anticipate other people will act in response to our own intended acts or words. These pressures may seem to arise from many different sources but in fact emerge primarily from our own past experiences and our command over the linguistic symbols of the culture. The way in which we internally symbolize and anticipate such pressures calls forth our responses to them. In this process, they also become inseparably bound up with our motives for any proposed course of action, so that motivation can only be understood by relating it to our conceptions of other people's expectations of our behavior. Motives are, therefore, always socially grounded.

The sociologist's major interest becomes one of making sense of or understanding the world retrospectively by describing the typical patterns of choice that operate and by showing the relationship between these patterns and the methods of their production. The importance of precisely predicting the future in analogous ways to natural scientific predictions recedes if this perspective is adopted. As Gibson Winter (1966) says:

The social world is dynamic whereas the grasp of that world in human science is fixed. Human action looks forward in its projects; human science looks backward to grasp the meaning of human action in terms of the past. This characteristic of human science marks its limits as a predictive and controlling discipline; human science talks about the future only on the assumption of continuity of past patterns of action. On the other hand, the value of human science arises from its explication of the conditions of human projects, bringing to consciousness many aspects of the social world which lie hidden from view and identifying regularities which give relative predictability to the social world (p. 121).

Such a perspective has many ramifications for both the conceptual and methodological problems of sociology and particularly for the kinds of statements and interpretations the sociologist wants and feels he is able to make about social relationships. His concern is to offer certain kinds of interpretations of social processes rather than to make precise statistical predictions about the future. Abandoning the precise predictive role may also impinge directly on the social and political importance accorded to sociological interpretations and methods, thus changing commonsense understandings of the nature and aims of sociology.

Advantages of the alternative perspective

The most important advantages of adopting this particular sociological perspective for the analysis of crime and delinquency can now be drawn together and summarized.

First, some of the serious value problems of traditional criminology are overcome; the subject matter is no longer defined for the investigator by existing legal norms and the mechanisms of the penal system. His field of study is defined by the norms and values of his discipline rather than by the existing legal norms of the society. The questions the investigator asks will only occasionally coincide with those asked by the society, and as soon as he explicitly tries to answer the society's questions, the sociologist runs the risk of tying himself to the values of powerful social groups and becoming a political instrument of those in power rather than an analyst.

Second, placing the study of crime and delinquency into the mainstream of sociology widens the perspective on crime and opens up the possibility of new levels of understanding. Moreover, sociology itself stands to gain from this assertion that crime is a social process, for the aim is to improve sociological understanding and not to solve social problems.

Third, and related to the last point, the sociological perspective stresses the similarity between criminal and other actions in society. Far from emphasizing the difference between criminal and noncriminal acts and thereby treating the criminal as an isolated phenomenon excluded from society, this approach draws out the similarities between crime and other social processes. By placing the study of crime in the wider context of social deviance, the analysis of the processes that generate other forms of deviance, such as mental illness, narcotic addiction, or professional misconduct, may give new insights into criminal behavior. Study of the processes that are common to the generation and maintenance of different types of social deviance leads to fresh perspectives on particular forms of deviance such as crime.

Fourth, by dropping a causal orientation, the hard determinism of many previous approaches is abandoned, and alternative ways of interpreting the problem of responsibility are proposed. This fulfills two purposes: It reasserts the importance of the philosophical underpinnings of sociology and points to the necessity of examining the basic assumptions about man on which sociology and criminology rest;

it asserts the inseparability of sociological theories or perspectives from research methods and practices that are too often treated as separate, independent parts of the discipline. Inevitably the emphasis on choice goes hand in hand with a very conscious realization of the dynamic nature of social life and moves the sociologist toward focusing on social processes and interaction patterns rather than the presentation of a static picture of social life that characterizes not only traditional criminology but also much sociology. Crime is no longer seen as "objectively given" but becomes, in the terms of Rubington and Weinberg (1968), "subjectively problematic;" that is, the very processes by which certain acts are defined and labeled as criminal and the consequences of such processes are viewed as constituted by the members' meanings. The negotiation of such meanings is always to some extent problematic for the participants themselves, while the sociologist faces the problem of the relationship between his observations as a nonparticipant (the meanings of the events from the "outside" in terms of his interests) and the "interior" view of the participants. The one-sidedness of earlier approaches with their restricted focus on the official deviant is replaced by a concern with the processes through which deviance is produced; this necessarily involves all of us.

The fifth advantage is related to the subjectively problematic nature of the processes studied by the sociologist and points to new ways for investigating the production and utilization of official statistics on crime and the penal system. Industrial societies annually produce a mass of criminal statistics used by the press, by politicians, by the public and all too frequently by criminologists and sociologists to draw general conclusions about the changing patterns of crime in a society, and by extension, about the society's changing moral climate. Such data, when viewed from the alternative perspective, become problematic in themselves and cannot be accepted as givens. They do not necessarily reflect "real" trends in the amount and form of crime in a society; they are seen rather as arising out of the very complex processes of interaction between offenders, victims, members of the public, and formal agencies of social control. Sociologists view these very processes as problematic and requiring investigation.

Official statistics are viewed not as mirror reflections or approximations of the "real" patterns of a society's crime but as the routine products of official organizations, which among other things, provide for their own accountability through statistics (for an elaboration of these points see Cicourel and Kitsuse, 1963a; and Garfinkel, 1967, Ch. 6). The apparently unequivocal patterns presented in official statistics, which provide a public with materials for incorporation into any "societal reaction" to crime, arise from complex and typically publicly hidden sifting and selecting processes and conflicting official requirements.

Illustrations of how some of these sifting processes are managed are provided in an excellent study of police work. Bittner's (1967) study of police "peace-keeping" practices in a skid row district shows that in peace-keeping work where there is both enormous freedom given to police and few official guides to assist them in their work; policemen quickly develop typical recipes for handling the multitude of problems they face. The informal recipes are based on extensive personal knowledge of the area and its inhabitants; one is judged to be a "good" skid row policeman by one's peers to the extent that one learns to follow these recipes. The recipes provide guides for handling the great discretion given to police in their peace-keeping work and display the situated character of the ways abstract legal norms are made to fit particular cases.

Finally, if the implications of this perspective for social policy in relation to crime and delinquency are considered, they may suggest why the programs of prevention, punishment, or treatment that have been directed without exception at the individual offender have signally failed in their aims of change. The sociological perspective suggests that major changes in the structure of social relationships (such as the abolition of private property) would be required to effect radical changes in the patterns of crime and delinquency in a society. Even assuming that such structural changes were to occur, crime would not disappear but would rather change its character. The impossibility of eliminating crime is a taken-for-granted canon of the sociological perspective. In relation to the kinds of social changes that might be required to alter the character and amount of crime in a society, it must be emphasized that such changes are of a political nature, and it is not part of the sociologist's task to make recommendations about social change, for the form of such recommendations will depend on the individual's personal values. The sociologist can only pose the questions and dilemmas for society and not the answers, for the latter will only emerge through political action and processes.

If these are some of the advantages and justifications for such a perspective, it is important to say something about the limiting features of its claims and aims.

Limiting features of the interactionist perspective

A feature of the recommended perspective that underlies all the work to be done within it and must preface subsequent discussion in this book concerns the role of the sociologist's concepts ("ideal" terms). The starting point for sociological analysis and, therefore, writing is that sociological descriptions never provide a simple mirror-image or reflection of the world, so that the frequent sociological claim to have portrayed the world "as it really is" is laid aside. All sociological description is seen as necessarily selecting only some things from social reality, the selection being guided by the founding assumptions of the particular perspective. These assumptions and concomitant selections necessarily display a sociologist's commitment to one way of making sociological sense of the forms of social order he observes. Because of the selectivity and partiality, the world is necessarily *transformed* in sociological descriptions. Unfortunately the "ideal" orders in sociological theories or descriptions are treated typically as revelations of underlying determinate orders that were somehow "in the world" before the sociological work and thought that produed them; it is as if these ideal orders were somehow independent of the ways sociologists constructed them.

The perspective espoused here treats sociological descriptions not as revelations of an objective world but as *possible* ways of seeing or reading social relationships. These "possible worlds" are the outcome of reconstructive work by sociologists and if we are to understand the human meanings of these possible worlds, we must locate the principles, rules, and methodic practices followed in this reconstructive work. Only then can we appreciate the transformations of the world sociological writing displays. A sociology that pays deep attention to its own origins and to the methods of its production and tries to make these explicit and available for a reader is being authentically reflexive. The development of a sociology that does not claim some kind of privileged status for its accounts (as better than or more objective than other kinds of accounts) but presents them as possible ways of viewing the social world has profound consequences for the social and political uses of sociology and for its claims to scientific status. Such a sociology also makes heavy demands on its readers, for it reminds them that to understand sociological descriptions necessarily requires work on their part; it is equally important for the reader to be reflexive about the intellectual work *he* is required to do to see the world through the *same* eyes as the sociologist whose work he reads. The reader must ask himself what *he* needs to know, what methods *he* brings to the text to produce some kind of congruence between his perception and the worlds available in the sociological text. In fact, the interpretive work required of a reader to make sense of a text rules out sociologists' claims to have provided objective, context-free descriptions. A reader necessarily relies on tacit knowledge for making some kind of sense of a text.

Thus in reading *this* text, the reader is asked not to treat the concepts used as offering mirror images of some assumedly independent social reality. My invitation is rather to treat the enterprise of reading as a collaboration in which the text is nothing without the reader's willing agreement to cooperate with the writer in the silent co-production of a possible world. The ensuing arguments and the concepts employed within them are rhetorical invitations to other alternative possible standpoints. My only aim in bringing to self-consciousness that which in some sense we "know" already and re-presenting it for the reader's attention is to encourage the reader to make the products of these shifts in perspective and self-consciousness relevant to his or her own life situation.

Apart from this background feature of the perspective, some substantive issues relate specifically to the conceptualization of deviance that might be useful to consider. A major difficulty seems to be that of the almost unlimited scope of the perspective; placing crime and delinquency within the much more inclusive study of social deviance creates interrelated difficulties for theorizing and researching. Given the ubiquity of norms and hence of deviance from them, some limitation of the area of study is called for if the study of deviance is to retain any coherence. Cohen's definition of deviance as norm-violating behavior is too general and requires modification. Some limitations on the scope of the interactionist perspective or some breakdown of the field into substantive areas of study according to the similarities in the deviance-generating processes is called for. For example, while parallels in the processes involved in cheating at cards and large-scale company frauds might be difficult to draw, the similarities in our labeling, processing and institutionalization of mentally ill persons and criminals and delinquents are much more obvious. Criteria for meaningfully subdividing the vast amorphous area of social deviance must be developed; such criteria might be defined by questions concerning how generally the norms being violated are held, whether the norms are supposed to apply to everybody in a society and are formally enforceable like the criminal law or they apply to only small select groups and are informally enforceable, and whether the identified deviant may be taken out of circulation or he is always allowed to remain within the community. If the analogies between deviance in different kinds of situations are to be meaningful rather than empty and naive, the main parameters of deviance must be defined and the field of study subdivided accordingly.

One such approach which attempts to limit the use of the term social deviance and to give it more clarity is offered by Lofland (1969). Taking the nation-state or total society as his reference point, he sees deviance as one kind of social conflict. He differentiates types of conflict according to criteria relating to the character and relations of parties in conflict and distinguishes deviance from simple nonconformity, civil uprising or disorder, social movements, civil war and mainstream party politics. He thus narrows the definition of deviance down in these terms:

> Deviance is the name of the conflict game in which individuals or loosely organized small groups, with little power are strongly feared by a well organized, sizable minority or majority who have a large amount of power. . . .
>
> A primary indicator of "this type of conflict called deviance" in a total society is, then, the existence of state rulings and corresponding enforcement mechanisms that provide for the possibility of forceably removing actors from civil society, either by banishment, annihilation, or incarceration. . . . Deviance is rule violation only in the limited sense that it involves violating the rules of relatively large minorities or majorities who are powerful, well organized, and highly fearful of individuals or loosely organized or small groups who lack power (pp. 14, 18, 19).

Lofland's approach overcomes the difficulties of Cohen's all-inclusive definition of deviance. Yet his category of deviance is still sufficiently broad to provide a basis for comparing apparently very different forms of deviance, like crime, mental illness, narcotic addiction, or even physical disability.

A further difficulty with the interactionist perspective arises from defining what is "normal." As suggested earlier, the study of deviance requires a concomitant concern with conformity, for before one can effectively define and describe what is deviant, one must have clear definitions of the norms from which deviance occurs. It is easy enough to assume, for example, in the case of crime and delinquency, that the normal is defined by the criminal law, but in practice this assumption may be entirely misplaced; normal behavior can only be defined as that which actually occurs and is seen as acceptable under the circumstances by the actors. The abstract principles embodied in the criminal law tell us little about the actual values that guide behavior in concrete everyday situations. While in traditional crimi-

nology assumptions were made about the norms, in the
alternative perspective defining the normal goes hand in
hand with defining the abnormal or the deviant; both are
problematic. It may be just as difficult in many situations to
define what is normal as it is to define what is deviant. This
may be particularly the case with criminal behavior, which
of necessity involves acts in which the actors generally try
to keep their identities a secret; even when nonparticipants
are "in the know," elaborate methods may be utilized to
preserve their silence. Perhaps in these circumstances it is
not so surprising that the criminologist abandoned the
study of actual norms and behaviors and restricted himself
to studying the failed offender. The most difficult problem
faced by the investigator of deviance is to define and describe the actual normal values and behavior of any individual or social group as opposed to the "respectable"
values offenders lay over their "unrespectable" activities.

The criteria of normality, then, are the criteria of *members themselves* and not of the sociologists, whose descriptive task is to reveal members' routine practices that index
"business as usual," that events are "as they should be,"
"unremarkable," and "alright until further notice." Members' ways of displaying the unremarkable character of
some events are indexes of the production of normal circumstances.

This leads directly to the third and conceivably the most
crucial problem facing the deviance perspective—the development and methodological styles appropriate to the
assumptions and concepts of this approach. If for the purposes of understanding and interpretation, the perspective
lays greatest emphasis on the meanings through which the
social world is constituted and on the processes of social
interaction, that is, on the dynamic character of social life,
the methodological problem is one of using methods that
reveal the socially organised character of meaning and give

access to interaction processes of interest. The social construction of meanings and interaction processes may not be easily elicited or observed in many areas of deviance. Restriction to the established and most common techniques of sociological research may give only a very limited and partial understanding of the processes of deviance, for they are unable to strip off the mask of respectability with which much deviance is covered.

A further limitation to the traditional techniques of sociological investigation is that they present relatively static pictures of social life, whereas the present perspective requires a focus on processes and social dynamics. Typically, the sociologist's research techniques center around the use of various kinds of interview methods involving the use of questionnaires and schedules and the analysis of organizationally produced records and data; less frequently used are content analyses of written documents such as letters, newspapers, magazines, or books. The least frequently used style of research, namely observation in which the observer typically lives in the milieu of or closely observes the activities of the group he is investigating, is the one that seems most likely to provide the sociologist with the most relevant material.

This style of participant and nonparticipant observation is particularly appropriate to the study of deviance in which the investigator's problem is to understand those very processes and meanings the deviant and those working both with and against him invariably attempt to conceal from prying eyes. The social distance that usually exists between deviant or official and researcher may be reduced through their acceptance of the investigator in their milieu; however it may take considerable time for sufficient trust to build up to affect this reduction. In comparison with other methods, this style of research has been under-used in sociology, and until recently there have been only a few studies in the area of deviance that typify this approach (see Whyte, 1966; Liebow, 1967; and Polsky, 1967, for useful discussions of the value of this approach; more recently Douglas, 1970c, 1972, provides several examples of contemporary work in a variety of contexts).

When it has been done, it has invariably laid bare levels of meaning that would have been unobtainable through the conventional sociological research techniques; at the same time such descriptions have a vividness that contrasts favorably with much arid sociological research reportage. Insofar as this kind of researcher is concerned, like any other sociologist, with the typical rather than the unique and providing he is honest enough to record his own feelings and responses as well as those of his subjects, it is suggested that these techniques must be integrated more effectively into sociology and must be seen not merely as subsidiary techniques but as essential and viable methodological styles (Bruyn, 1966).

In fact, the influences of the interactionist perspective and a phenomenologically oriented sociology have produced a rapid growth of studies in the field of deviance which take seriously members' own accounts of their activities and the observation of the production of deviance. Far from apologizing for their approach, recent authors are arguing increasingly for the necessity of this kind of research and the materials it produces (see also J. Douglas, 1970b).

Thus the main methodological problem for this perspective are to develop methods that give access to those routine activities of members that are both ignored by and unreachable through conventional research procedures, and to make these very methods of material gathering and analysis (the observer's work) as problematic as the substantive analysis itself. The tackling of this second problem would contribute powerfully to the development of a reflexive sociology (see O'Neill, 1972, esp. Ch. 14).

Relevant questions in the alternative perspective

At the most basic level, the sociologist must answer the question: Is crime or, more generally, deviance in some form inevitable, that is, is it an inherent feature of social organization? Certainly all the empirical evidence points to the universality of crime, but does this necessarily mean that crime is logically bound up with the conditions necessary for society to exist? This issue of the normality of crime is a fundamental one for sociologists, for in the way in which it is answered has implications both for the kind of explanations of crime that can be proposed and also for utopian beliefs about the possibility of eliminating crime.

More specifically, the second kind of question asks how we can understand the particular patterns of crime that characterize any given society. There are two distinct steps to be followed in answering this question. A description of the character of the society's crime must precede any attempted interpretation, and such a description may not be easy, for the deviance student brackets the picture of crime presented in the official criminal and penal statistics. Only if this problem of description can be adequately overcome can the question be asked: Why this pattern as opposed to any other? Answers to this question would always rest on certain philosophical, sociological, and psychological assumptions about the nature of man and the nature of the phenomena sociologists study, but essentially the task of interpretation would be to show the relationships between criminal and deviant phenomena and other social processes and institutions. In effect, the sociologist argues that an understanding of crime can only come from a demonstration of how it is bound up with other aspects of social life. Far from treating it as a separate, autonomous entity, the sociologist attempts to show how the pattern of crime is inextricably intertwined with the network of social relationships comprising the society. The distribution and pattern of crime in the society will suggest those aspects of the social structure towards which the sociologist's analysis will be primarily directed.

The third fundamental question is, in practice, closely bound up with the previous one; however, because it has received little attention in sociological interpretations of crime and delinquency until recently, its importance should be emphasized. The question asks about the attempts to control and regulate crime in a society: What are the dominant processes of social control in relation to crime? In posing this question, the sociologist would investigate the processes by which the criminal is selected, identified, labeled and punished and through which the society attempts to effect changes in criminals and to prevent crime. In fact, the answers to this question would complement the answers obtained to the previous question, for the deviance theorist would argue that there is a dialectical relationship between the amount and character of deviance in a society and the attempts to prevent and control such deviance. Rates of deviance are a product of the complex interactions between those who, for whatever reasons, come to be perceived as deviants and the agents of social control; changes on the one side of the equation will call forth changes on the other. The sociologist's problem is to describe the ever-changing relationship between the two halves of the equation.

Finally, and underpinning each of these questions that are largely concerned with general social processes and issues of social structure, the perspective poses questions designed to clarify sociological understanding of individual projects and courses of action and to place these within their social context. An understanding of the ubiquity of deviance, the particular forms it takes in different social structures and its relationship to social control processes rests on the study of the typical structures of social meaning at the face-to-face level of analysis. The perspective sees the meaning structures of individuals as created, maintained, modified or drastically changed in ongoing processes of interaction and individual interpretation. The inherently creative individual is viewed in his socially meaningful actions as constantly involved in the creation, maintenance, and validation of a self, an identity. Thus sociological analysis and understanding of deviance and control at the interpersonal level, recognizing creativity, attempts to place individual actions within the context of the socially typical. Some of the kinds of analytical issues concerning the self and face-to-face interaction which are seen as important in this perspective, such as the distinction between primary and secondary deviation, the development of deviant identities, or the move into a deviant group are discussed in more detail in Chapter 4. Understanding the human meaning of deviance and control at the interpersonal or intentional level arguably poses the greatest conceptual and methodological challenges to the sociologist.

3

The Paradox of Social Control
and
the Normality of Crime

Introduction

This chapter discusses some aspects of the ubiquitous character of the social deviance and social reactions to it. All known societies have socially defined rules, individuals who break them, and ways of dealing with those rule-breakers who are caught. Two important complementary interpretations of aspects of this universality—by Durkheim (1950) and Mead (1918)—provide a key part of the conceptual base of the interactionist perspective, and the analytical questions about crime and its control that are suggested by these interpretations are very different in character from those of traditional criminology. Each author deals with different aspects of the relationship between, first, the character of social organization and the definition of crime and, second, the individual and the society of which he is a member. Their analyses of the social sources of the rules outlawing certain behaviors as deviant provide a basis for the study of deviance within particular societies. A question that arises in Durkheim's (1950) analysis concerns the possibility of a society without crime. The answers Durkheim provides to this question are integral to his discussion of the normality of crime. As the idea of the normality of crime is a central tenet of the interactionist perspective and at the same time a contradiction of much common-sense thinking about crime, it is worth considering this question in some detail.

Rules as providing for the possibility of crime

In trying to answer the question, "Is a society without crime possible?" we have to move away from culture-bound definitions of which actual behaviors constitute crime in any given society to a consideration of crime as an abstract category. Instead of thinking of crime, for example, in terms of those particular behaviors typically outlawed by the legal systems of industrial societies, we have to turn to those features of crime that are common to many different types of societies, from the institutionally complex to the apparently simpler societies. The strands binding the many different societal definitions of crime together are the common social processes involved and not the diverse contents of what is actually defined as crime. The abstract category of crime becomes those behaviors outlawed by societies' laws or customs and, if undertaken and detected, call forth certain responses from the societies' agents of social control. These controlling responses are public in character, usually of a ritual or ceremonial nature, and are carried out by agents who claim to represent the communities' dominant interests.

This tells us that there is no such thing as "natural crime;" there are no behaviors that are always crimes *in themselves* irrespective of cultural definitions. Crime comprises those classes of behavior that, if committed in certain social contexts and ways, are defined as crime by the laws or customs of the society.

Thus, that which is seen as simply *behavior* by an ob-

server who "external" to the culture being observed (and
as such is describable to the observer's "objective" terms),
may have various meanings as *social conduct* or *action*
to the participants in the culture. We may all agree that A
has killed B (behavior) but differ as to whether the act was
murder (social conduct or action).

Our problem as sociological observers is to describe
members' methodic practices for transforming "behavior"
into "social action." In the study of criminal deviance, this
requires us to move away from a reliance on legal ideals as
found in formal statutes and to focus on the situated character of the production of deviance. Legal ideals are made
to fit particular behaviors (thereby transforming them into
social action) through processes of interpretation in particular situations.

This approach again emphasizes the cultural and temporal relativity of the definition of crime and also lends
support to the substitution of the concept of deviance for
that of crime; use of the deviance approach directs attention away from culture-bound definitions of crime to the
general social processes involved in publicly outlawing and
sanctioning deviant acts and individuals.

That no behavior is inherently criminal can be demonstrated by showing that even those acts that our society
considers to be the most heinous crimes not only cease to be
defined as crime but may become praiseworthy acts if they
are performed in certain circumstances. For example, killing is legitimated on a vast scale in time of war or when it
is performed on our behalf by the public executioner. In
both cases, many people, such as pacifists and abolitionists,
would define even such officially legitimated killings as
murder in terms of their personal values. These grave dis-
putes at the level of public debate concerning the meanings
attached to the act of killing illustrate the importance of
analyzing actual social definitions of crime rather than

relying on the abstract letter of the law. Similarly, in our law, for killing as for any other crime, mitigating circumstances can dramatically reduce the severity of society's reactions to functionally equivalent behaviors. What we might define as child murder was seen as perfectly legitimate by the Spartans when they tested the survival capacity of their newly born infants by placing them on the frosty roof for a night. Rape, by definition, cannot exist within marriage, although the behavior itself—forced intercourse—may be functionally equivalent to a comparable behavior committed outside the bounds of marriage and given the official label of rape.

Crime in the abstract, as an "ideal" category, would thus comprise all those acts in any society that are thought to be infringements of the official rules of that society; but empirically, at the level of official or public knowledge, crime is that collection of acts that have been officially located, described, and given a legal label. Because of the importance of legal processing in industrial societies as the arbiter of what crime is and who the criminal is, the first category consists of that which is *possibly* crime; this is transformed into a body of actual criminal events through the actions of a social audience that produces the official knowledge of crime.

Official rules are reflections of a range of values that are more or less strongly held within the society, either by most people for most of the time or by smaller interest groups that are sufficiently well organized politically to enforce their values through the official rules and the official agencies of social control. The question of the political organization of minority interest groups is especially important in relation to law maintenance and law reform in industrial societies where many government decisions may be the results of conflicts of interest between competing pressure groups. In England, for example, recent changes in the law relating to abortion reflect the compromise of interests reached between organized competing pressure groups such as the Roman Catholic Church, the medical profession, and the Abortion Law Reform Association. Definitions of the content of crime are undergoing constant changes and subtle modifications, and even though the laws themselves may not be changed, the meanings given to the law may shift in their emphases; such changes in meaning may be observed in the cases where laws remain on the statute book but are rarely invoked or enforced. This would suggest that the content of the official statutes in any point in time may provide only a moderate introductory guide to the patterns of values that are actually held to be publicly enforceable at that time; if we are looking for those values, they can only be reflected in the actual patterns of deviantly defined behaviors and the controlling responses they evoke. These patterns of actual control activities are the direct reflection of those values that are important to the society or the organized segments of society, and beliefs about what is important undergo constant change.

Clearly crime, then, can exist only if there are some publicly acknowledged and enforced rules of conduct in a society. If we could find or logically conceive of a society either without rules at all or with a set of rules that *everybody kept all the time,* the view of crime as inevitable or normal would have to be rejected. However, if such a society is both nonexistent and inconceivable, apart from in our fantasies, crime must be viewed as a normal phenomenon, as something that is inevitably present wherever society is found.

Two sociologists from very different intellectual traditions offer complementary perspectives on this issue and provide the logic on which rests a taken-for-granted tenet of contemporary deviance theorists, namely, that crime must be viewed as a normal phenomenon because it is bound up with the very conditions of existence of society. Let us consider their discussions briefly.

Durkheim's discussion of the normality of crime

The French sociologist Emile Durkheim was the first sociologist to deal theoretically with the question of the normality of crime. In *The Rules of Sociological Method,* first published in 1895, Durkheim (1950) argued that the sociologist could establish the normality of any social phenomenon by answering two complementary questions, the first of which was empirical and the second theoretical. The empirical question asked: Is the particular social phenomenon to be found in every known society? If the answer to this was "yes," the theoretical question was then asked: Is it logically bound up with the conditions necessary for group life? For Durkheim, these were the two essential criteria of normality: The first, being simply a statistical operation, would demonstrate the ubiquity of the phenomenon and the second would be the logical explanation of this ubiquity. The example Durkheim chose to illustrate this method was crime.

First, he pointed out in answer to the empirical question that every known society possessed both rules outlawing certain behaviors that offended "strongly held collective sentiments" (p. 67) and individuals who occasionally did offend such sentiments and drew "upon themselves penal repression." The ubiquity of crime was empirically indisputable, but how was it logically inevitable and therefore necessary?

To answer this second question Durkheim focused on the relationship between the individual consciousness of the members of a society and the collective sentiments embodied in the criminal law. His argument makes the following points:

1. For any category of criminal behavior to disappear completely from a society there would have to be unanimity of feeling amongst all members of the society towards the behavior. All would have to feel sufficiently intensely about it to rule out the possibility of its committal.

2. Given this increase in intensity sufficient to prevent the occurrence of certain acts (for whatever reasons it occurred), crime would not disappear but would simply change its form; the changes in the intensity of the unanimous collective sentiments would mean that those behaviors that were previously regarded as "simple moral faults" (p. 68) would take on the status of crimes in the changed society. In Durkheim's own words:

> Imagine a society of saints, a perfect cloister of exemplary individuals. Crimes, properly so called, will there be unknown; but faults which appear venial to the layman will create there the same scandal that the ordinary offense does in ordinary consciousness (pp. 68–69).

3. The elimination of dissent (deviance or crime) from society is impossible because it would require absolute uniformity of consciousness among all the individuals in a society. Such a uniformity of consciousness is precluded by the nature of consciousness itself. It is not even possible for two individuals, let alone all the members of a society, even to approach identity of consciousness. Disagreement is built into the fact of the uniqueness of individual experience and so therefore is the inevitability of deviance.

An English sociologist, Wilkins (1964), uses the statistical normal curve distribution to illustrate his theory of deviance, and a modification of his use of the normal curve may help to illustrate the logic of Durkheim's argument. In the figure (p. 73), the area under the curve represents the volume of social acts of the society; in the motto of an English national newspaper: "All of life is here." The

original curve imposed on the baseline (AC) might be
taken to represent activity in society as we know it, with
actions ranging from the most honest act (A) to the most
heinous crime (C) and with the law (B) cutting off as
illegal a proportion (X) of the acts performed in the society. To eliminate crime as we know it, the baseline would
have to move up to (A_1C_1), following the heightened intensity of the collective sentiments; however, it is clear that
there are still extreme forms of behavior in the new society
that are outlawed following the increased intensity, so the
legal cut off point moves to B_1 and the outlawed acts become
X_1. Following each heightening of intensity, one group of
acts disappears altogether to be replaced by another group
which attract similar penal repression; note that the volume
of acts in society is getting smaller and smaller following
each heightening of the intensity of the collective sentiments. Finally, with the coincidence of A_n, B_n, and C_n, we
arrive at the ultimate situation of no social action. In other
words, the more behaviors that are eliminated through
the increasing intensity of the collective sentiments, the less
action there is in the society. Taken to its ultimate absurd-
ity the argument suggests that the collective sentiments at
the apex of the curve and their intensity would outlaw all
action in society, at which point society would cease to exist.

The logic of this argument leads Durkheim to conclude
that a society without some form of crime or deviance is a
contradiction in terms; deviance, in other words, is bound
up with the conditions necessary for society to exist and
results from the unique nature of individual consciousness.
Naturally this argument goes against many of our accepted
beliefs and hopes about deviance and its punishment, treatment, and prevention; it also serves as a salutary warning
to the builders of utopias that the elimination of all forms
of deviance cannot be achieved. Accepting the normality
of deviance means, as Durkheim also pointed out, accepting

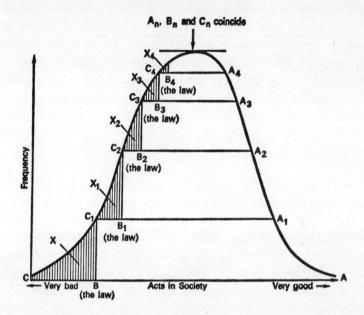

its usefulness or rather recognizing that the collective sentiments that are sufficiently flexible to allow for criminal deviance by this very flexibility allow also for the possibility of social change through individual originality. The flexibility that allows the criminal to exist also allows the political, religious, artistic, scientific, or immediately practical innovator to coexist. All these individuals or groups are deviating from the culturally accepted ways of thinking and acting and are putting forward alternatives to existing beliefs and practices.

It must be emphasized that Durkheim was talking about the normality of crime and criminality and not about the normality of the individual criminal. These are two analytically distinct questions which are leveled at different phenomena; the question of the normality of crime is answered at the cross-cultural level of analysis and refers to total societies, whereas the question of the normality of

the criminal can only be meaningfully posed about individual criminals *within* a given society. As mentioned
earlier, the criteria of individual normality and abnormality are culturally specific so that the definitions of individual criminals as normal or abnormal can only be understood
by examining the criteria of normality in that society.

Mead's discussion of the social organization of judicial punishment

A complementary perspective is provided in an essay by
the American philosopher and social psychologist George
Herbert Mead entitled "The Psychology of Punitive Justice" (1918). In this essay, while he is not explicitly
concerned with normality as such, Mead perceptively
discusses the symbolic meaning of the criminal law and
punitive justice to members of a society. The characteristic
societal response to the criminal is to punish him, and Mead
attempts to account for the particular forms of social organization that reflect society's hostility towards the criminal
and their implications. The two most frequent justifications
for punishment of the criminal are retribution and deterrence.

Initially we justify punishment by arguing that the criminal deserves to be punished simply because he has committed the crime; by committing the crime he has given
members of society the right to inflict retributive punishment. The justification of deterrence is one of social expedience, and through it we decide the severity and form
of the punishment; the emphasis shifts from simple retribution to the idea of prevention through deterrence. We
believe that we can effect some kind of commensurability
between the severity of the punishment, the assumed deterrent fear we believe it inspires in both the offender
himself and future potential offenders, and the extent to

which we feel aggrieved by the criminal's actions. At first sight then, Mead argues, our punishment of the criminal seems to reflect these two justifications of deterrence and retribution, and yet these two principles are insufficient to explain the socially organized reactions to the criminal. If these were the only principles involved, the kind of penal process that would emerge would be some kind of lynch or mob law that would inevitably operate in a random way. Mead finds the key to the problem of understanding our punishment of the criminal in what he calls the "majesty of the law," in the "assumed solemnity of criminal court procedure," and in the "supposedly impartial and impersonal character of justice." In other words, he focuses on the public ritual and drama of the criminal trial, which he sees as reflecting the "theoretically impartial enforcement of the common will" and through which justice is to be done "though the heavens fall."

He likens criminal court procedure to a battle between the contending parties; the very nature of this battle serves to define and reinforce our emotional attitudes towards the two parties for "the emotions called out are the emotions of battle." In this battle the law is presented as both the defender of the community and the attacker of the enemies of the community so that insofar as each member at all identifies with the wider community, he sees the punitive process defending him and attacking the offender on his behalf. The basis of the criminal law, as reflected in the drama of the penal process, appears to lie in its dual purpose of, first, arousing in law-abiding members of the community "the inhibitions which make rebellion impossible for them" and, second, of stigmatizing the offender either by removing him from the community in the extreme case or by some lesser form of stigmatization arising from the ritual public labeling process. Even for minor infractions of the law the public nature of the judicial process

that provides the offender with an official criminal record
serves to label and stigmatize him effectively as an enemy
of the community. Such stigmatization may have far-
reaching implications for the offender's identity and moral
career.

The conflict nature of the confrontation between the law,
which protects abstract rights of the community members,
and the criminal suggests that the hostile attitude reflected
in retributive and deterrent punishments is inescapable.
Indeed, Mead goes on to suggest that this attitude of hostility cannot be reconciled with the principles of treatment
and reform of the criminal; the aims of punishment and
eradication of the causes of crime seem to be mutually exclusive. In Mead's terms, "as long as the social organization
is dominated by the attitude of hostility the individuals or
groups who are the objects of this organization will remain
enemies. It is quite impossible psychologically to hate the
sin and love the sinner" (p. 228). He thus calls into question the logic of the current attempts of the penal systems
of industrial societies to combine punishment with techniques for changing criminals. There is an irreconcilable
conflict between punishment and treatment.

The main result of this attitude of hostility towards the
criminal is, Mead concludes, a sense of social solidarity:
community members who otherwise have quite divergent
individual interests unite in their solidarity against the
common enemy; they submerge their differences and unite
in their hostility towards the law-breaker. Indeed this sense
of social solidarity may be the crucial way of holding the
community together and of defining its limits; insofar as
the convicted criminal is responsible for this social solidarity by attracting public hostility towards himself, he seems
to be making a major contribution to preserving and defining the boundaries of the community. In fact, Mead does
not see the criminal as presenting a real threat to the per-

manence of the community, but he does see him as calling forth a social solidarity that continually serves to reaffirm and reinforce the community's values concerning members' rights and duties.

The idea that the criminal does not present a real threat to the structure of society perhaps requires some clarification. What Mead seems to imply is that the criminal is of necessity secretive and that the clandestine nature of his activities does not provide a basis from which radically to change the social structure; far from wishing to change social relationships through his activities, the criminal prefers to be devious within the existing social arrangements. He can never pose a real threat to the social structure because he is not offering a viable alternative; any social organization he does undertake in the course of his activities is concerned only with the isolated criminal project in hand, and he poses no major threat to structural arrangements. In contrast, the political rebel has as his central motivating force the desire to change the social structure so that while he may, of necessity, remain secretive in the early stages of his activities, he can only achieve his aims by eventually obtaining some kind of public support; he is forced at some stage to come out into the open if he is to succeed. For the criminal to step into the open and declare his intentions at any stage would be to invite disaster for his project. It seems then that the criminal prefers to work at the margins of the existing community boundaries rather than consciously to attempt to redefine those boundaries. Conventional criminal activities are committed in spite of the law and not with a view to changing it.

In fact, the penal system treats many explicitly political rebels in the same way as it treats those found guilty of the more conventional criminal activities so that they may consider themselves inadvertently and wrongly labeled "criminal." The small minority of political criminals whose aim is to effect certain political changes by making their declarations of intent and actions public do pose a visible threat to the existing power structure, and if they step close to the margins of legitimate political protest, they immediately call onto themselves the punitive repression normally reserved for the secretive criminal. The main differences between the two types of criminals seem to lie therefore in their intentions and in the openness of their activities; the nature of these differences supports Mead's contention that the conventional criminal poses no real threat to the social structure.

The question of the tenuous distinction between "political" and "mundane" crime has been raised most powerfully by recent political events in which the traditional claim of criminal courts to be independent of and "above" political interests has been called into question by various groups. In his report on the "Politics of Protest," Skolnick (1969) shows how the courts, faced with riots and "mass disorders" shift their function from serving the ideals of the judicial establishment of guilt or innocence to contribute to riot control in a variety of ways; for example, high bonds are used to keep "rioters" off the streets. When the system is under pressure, new norms of judicial practice emerge that are grounded in situational contingencies rather than the principles of "ideal" judicial response; the courts typically adopt a law-enforcement perspective. Similarly, any arraigned individual who either openly calls into question the legitimacy of the court to try him or is publicly skeptical of the courts' capacity to mete out fair and equal criminal justice is thereby inviting us to become more critically self-conscious about what courts are doing in our name (for example, see *Tales of Hoffman,* Levine, McNamee, and Greenberg, 1970).

By focusing on the characteristics of the hostile attitude

to the criminal as reflected in the social meanings given to the criminal law and the punitive penal processes, Mead both complements and adds to Durkheim's discussion of the normality of crime. His analysis of the emergence of the processes of hostility, social solidarity, public labeling, and consequent stigmatization of the criminal suggests how the interaction between the criminal and the penal system confirms a community's moral boundaries by constantly defining and reaffirming what is permissible and what is not. These definitions and reaffirmations keep alive the sense of what the community means and is.

The unavoidable dilemma of whether to punish or attempt to change the criminal is also clearly stated by Mead. The attitude of hostility that results in punishment provides for the maintenance of a sense of a community's moral boundaries. It produces a group of "outsiders" (the punished and stigmatized). Hostility towards these outsiders precludes that empathy with their motivation, which would be necessary for an "adequate" understanding of their rule breaking; the punisher is unable to take the role of the rule breaker fully and see the world through his eyes —to see why he broke the rule. This inability to understand the offender and the concomitant hostility towards him results in attempts within the penal system to prevent him undertaking further rule breaking. Such attempts are predominantly punitive (deterrent) and occasionally therapeutic (reformative) in origin and impetus; but whichever predominates the importance of the offender's *own* reasons and grounds for his actions are subordinated to those issues, explanations, and remedies provided by the ideologies of the social controllers. Thus, for example, crime can be a product of moral failure to be eliminated by punishment and penance, or a product of mechanical learning to be eliminated by unlearning through aversion therapy or a product of an inner pathology or conflict to be eliminated by psychiatric or psychoanalytic technique, or product of subculture to be eliminated by intensive interaction in a self-help group of the offender's peers, and so on. In so far as these ideologies of explanation and remedy look to phenomena other than the existential commitments of the individual offender, they are providing positivist accounts that deny the human character of the offender's enterprise; in so doing they are covering and denying the relevance of the meaning of both the rule-breaking *and* the societal reaction to the offender himself. Any deterrence or reform that does occur in these circumstances is an inexplicable by-product of the societal reaction, for the meaning of the punishment or reform to the offender will be neither known nor looked for; the controllers' ideologies direct them to phenomena other than the meaning of *their* actions to those acted on in their assessment of the efficacy of their remedies. Positivist explanations (including those used by both social scientists and practitioners such as judges or psychiatrists) dehumanize the human grounds of deviant enterprises, while interactionist and phenomenological interpretations point to deviance and its control as human products, the intelligibility of which provides the subject matter for analysis. Contemporary penal systems reflect these ideological differences in explanations and remedies and are subject to a variety of conflicting pressures ranging from aggressive hostility to the criminal to demands for extensive penal reform. The "irrational equilibrium" (Conrad, 1965) penal systems maintain displays the precariousness with which they balance on the horns of the punishment versus change dilemma.

The problems or role conflicts facing social workers employed in the penal service epitomize this dilemma. Probation officers, for example, are first officers and servants of the criminal court; they are thus regarded by convicted offenders as punitive agents, and they may often be directly involved in the enforcement of the civil and criminal law. On the other hand, the ideology of social casework, in whose underlying principles probation officers are instructed during training, runs directly counter to the punitive principle. It rests on the building of a trusting relationship between caseworker and client with a view to helping the client to an understanding of his "problems" which would enable him to help himself. The "problems" diagnosed by casework ideology are typically derived from the untested and often untestable assumptions of psychoanalytic theory and may bear little relation to what the client would define as problematic. But the main point in this context is the conflict between the demands placed on the probation officer as a punitive servant of the court and the requirements of the professional social work ideology. Their irreconcilability illustrates the problems involved in trying to implement reformative or therapeutic measures based on certain kinds of understanding of "the problem" in a punitive setting.

Apart from his discussion of the normality of crime, Durkheim also provides an analysis of punishment which closely parallels that of Mead. His work *Moral Education*, published in 1925, includes an analysis of the role of punishment in the school in which several of his insights and hypotheses concerning punishment are generalizable to official punishment for infractions of the criminal law (Durkheim, 1961). He argues that the essential function of punishment is not simply retributive, nor is it to produce individual atonement, nor is it to deter the offender, but rather it is to demonstrate the inviolability of the rule broken by the offender. Thus, Durkheim argues, the pain produced in the punished offender is only an incidental repercussion of punishment, and the severe punishment of an act is only justifiable to the extent that it is necessary to make public disapproval of the act "utterly unequivocal."

Suffering is thus merely a secondary element in punishment and in some circumstances may be totally lacking, for the publicly observed punishment may not be experienced as suffering by the offender; an example of this might be probation for those offenders for whom it is a mere irritation. The crucial element in punishment, then, is the affirmation in the face of an offense of the rule that the offense denies. In Durkheim's words:

> If nothing happens to neutralize its effects a moral violation *demoralizes*. What must there be to rectify the evil thus produced? The law that has been violated must somehow bear witness that despite appearances it remains always itself, that it has lost none of its force or its authority despite the act that repudiated it. In other words, it must assert itself in the face of the violation and react in such a way as to demonstrate a strength proportionate to that of the attack against it. Punishment is nothing but this meaningful demonstration (p. 166).

Similar to Mead, Durkheim is arguing that evaluations of punishment that restrict their attention to its effects on individual offenders, as in traditional criminology, are missing its essential meaning. By pointing to the wider social meaning or function of punishment, Durkheim offers a range of hypotheses concerning the relationship between rule violation and punishment that have yet to be investigated by sociologists; for example, in discussing the kind of punishment system a school should set up, he outlines a theory of recidivism that fits well the experience of modern penal systems.

> All punishment, once applied, loses a part of its influence by the very fact of its application. What lends it authority, what makes it formidable, is not so much the misery that it causes as the moral discredit implied in the blame that it expresses. This feeling of moral sensitivity that stands guard against misdeeds is one of the most delicate of sentiments. It is not

strong, it is not completely itself, it lacks its full power of influence except among those for whom it has lost nothing of its
original purity. We often say that the first offense always
leads to others. This is because, once we have felt it, we are
less sensitive to this shame. Punishment has this very great
limitation of clashing with one of the chief resources of moral
life, and thus reducing its own efficacy in the future. It retains
all of its force only when it simply constitutes a threat. . . .
Punishment cannot but contribute to future lapses (pp. 198–
99).

It can be seen from these quotations that there is a certain
tension between Mead's and Durkheim's analyses of punishment. For Durkheim, hostility towards the rule-breaker
is not punishment's essential component, but punishment is
a principle demonstration of a rule's inviolability.

These analyses of Durkheim and Mead of the meaning of
deviance and attempts to control it require us to drop our
taken-for-granted assumptions about the effects of punishment and draw our attention towards the wider issues of
the social meanings attached to laws and their enforcement.

Implications of these ideas for
the analysis of deviance

Several American sociologists have developed the impli-
ations of Mead's idea about the peculiar character of
punitive justice and have emphasized different aspects.
Tannenbaum (1938) refers to the ritual character of the
criminal court as the "dramatization of evil" and sees this
very dramatization as contributing to the confirmation of
the criminal in his deviant role. In a similar way, Garfinkel
(1956) calls the court processing of the criminal a "status
degradation ceremony" in which the convicted offender's
civil status is dramatically removed and is publicly replaced
by the new identity and demoted status of "criminal."

More recently, Erikson (1962), echoing Durkheim, points out that the very institutions whose ostensible purpose is to correct the deviant seem much more likely to confirm him in his deviant role; our prisons, mental hospitals, juvenile detention centers, and other institutions for those excluded from conventional society provide ample opportunities for learning the "skills and attitudes of a deviant career, and often provoked them [the excluded] into employing these skills by reinforcing their sense of alienation from the rest of society." Indeed, in view both of the depressingly, if understandably, high rates of recidivism the ex-inmates of such institutions produce, and also concomitantly of the miniscule economic and human resources allocated to these institutions, Erikson questions whether we can consider the suppression of deviance to be their "real" function at all. If we were serious about the suppression of deviance, he asks, would we not devote much more energy and resources to the task? The writings of Tannenbaum, Garfinkel, Erikson, and others, then, all rest on Durkheim's and Mead's analyses of crime and society's responses to it, and each of them suggests in complementary ways that the very social processes apparently designed to reduce deviance ironically seem to produce and foster it.

We have now to consider how these complementary views of the normality of crime and deviance can be related to the perspective proposed in the previous chapter. It was suggested that an adequate understanding of crime or any social phenomenon can come only from an investigation of the typical social meanings individuals give to their situations and out of which they construct their actions. A major task is thus to examine how these typical social meanings emerge, are maintained, and change; the individual's consciousness and self-consciousness is placed at the center of this approach, and it is the product of the individual's consciousness upon which the sociologist draws to build up his patterns of typical social meanings. Clearly the basic unit of study is individual consciousness.

As we have seen, certain ideas about individual consciousness are indispensable to both Durkheim's and Mead's discussions. In Durkheim's analysis, at the most fundamental level it is the uniqueness of the individual's consciousness that precludes the possibility of a deviance-free society; moreover, his explanation of how crime, rather than disappearing, only changes its forms, rests on ideas about changing forms of consciousness. The universally experienced heightened sentiment which might rid society of one kind of criminal act serves at the same time to direct the equivalent opprobrium towards acts that previously had attracted only mild disapproval; the change in social consciousness redirects attention and defines new behaviors as criminal. Thus the nature of individual and social consciousness is fundamental to Durkheim's analysis. It is only through shared social meanings that some criminal acts disappear from society and others take their place.

Similarly, Mead's discussion of society's punitive reaction to crime as manifested in the penal system centers on the meanings given to crime and criminals by the members of the community. He shows how the criminal calls forth certain hostile responses and how these responses are crystallized and institutionalized in systems of punitive justice. The social meanings given to criminals and their acts, because of their hostile character, reduce the possibility of nonpunitive methods of change based on empathic understanding of the criminal. Control apparatus reflects the social meaning of crime and the criminal in a given society.

The other authors mentioned all give primacy in their discussions to the forms of consciousness that emerge from and reinforce our organizational processes for handling the convicted criminal. The ritual and systematic processes of branding, labeling, demoting, and excluding the criminal impinge on both the social meanings given to the criminal by members of the community and also, equally important, on the social meanings given by the criminal to his own acts and to himself. Such processes arise out of our initial hostility towards the criminal and in their turn effectively reinforce both our hostility and the criminal's view of himself as an outsider. The conscious social meanings thus given to crime and reflected in our systems of handling convicted criminals are all-important for understanding the complementary processes of deviance and control.

An essay by Christie (1968), comparing the changing uses of prison in four Scandinavian countries, neatly illustrates the value of comparative and historical materials in displaying the ways particular forms of punishment reflect changing social values. He shows, for example, how the changing meanings and importance of the deprivations that have typically been used as punishments (life, limb, time, money) impinge on the methods implemented in penal systems.

The implications of accepting the view that deviance is a normal phenomenon are considerable. Once it is realized that deviance in some form is a fundamental feature of any social group or society, the analytical problems change accordingly. By accepting the inevitability of deviance, the sociologist's attention is directed away from the search for causes of crime through the study of the biographies of individual convicted criminals and towards social processes and a society's structure of social meanings.

Although deviance as a social process is inherent in social organization, this is not to deny that at the individual level there are many different kinds and degrees of deviance that occur for many different reasons. The possible content of deviant processes in a society obviously depends on the structure of formal and informal rules in that society; in complex industrial societies, even if attention is restricted to the range of formal rules, such as the criminal and civil law, they impinge on every area of social life. Given the range of these rules and the situations they relate to, the origins of particular individual deviations are not reducible to a handful of underlying individual characteristics but are as broad as the range of human motivation itself; indeed, the same rule, such as a criminal law, may be broken for opposite reasons in different contexts. Shoplifting may variously be a game for schoolboys, an occupation and livelihood for one adult, and an occasional means of saving on the housekeeping expenses for another. Thus, part of the analytical task of the interactionist perspective is to clarify the typical social meanings of deviations and to place these in the context of the creation and enforcement of the rule being broken.

If deviance is inevitable, if it is inherent in the very nature of society, to seek to explain it in terms of either individual characteristics or determinate social factors is to blind oneself to its actual nature. Traditional criminology sought to do just that. Its theories and methods were based on the assumption that crime was the result of something within the individual convicted criminal and that by studying the latter, eventually the peculiar crime-producing individual characteristics would be located. These characteristics would be the causes, and once they were defined and located society could sift out those individuals who possessed them. Acceptance of the normality of deviance immediately requires a rejection of the traditional view and the substitution of a focus on social processes; it demands a recognition that deviance can be understood by an examination of the processes of interaction in which some members of a society are labeled as deviant by others and come to take on a deviant identity. This view argues that, while deviance itself is inevitable, the actual patterns of deviance in a society are problematic for the sociologist; it is the patterns and not the mere presence of deviance that require understanding.

These patterns are composed of typical social meanings; an understanding of crime in any society, therefore, requires the sociologist to locate both the social meanings that define crime, criminals, and social reactions to them in that society and also the processes through which such meanings emerge, change, and are maintained.

In opposition to earlier work that sought to explain crime as abnormal or pathological and criminals as special kinds of people, the interactionist perspective recommends that sociologists shift their focus of attention to other phenomena; through studying the *ordinary* and *routine* processes of social life we can clarify the origins of those forms of behavior we characterize as crime as well as the sources and uses of the characterizations themselves.

4

The Analysis of Crime
from an
Interactionist Perspective

Introduction

The discussion in this and the remaining chapters focuses on crime in contemporary industrial societies; the distinctive patterns of crime and societal reactions to them that characterize industrial societies can be understood only by relating them to the surrounding structures of social meaning and social processes. Such structures and processes are very different in character from those found in what have traditionally been called simple societies. It is in industrial societies also that particular patterns of criminal behavior have been publicly defined as "serious social problems" requiring certain sorts of public action to reduce the problem. We have already noted that this public definition of certain forms of crime and delinquency as important social problems was one of the main reasons so much time and energy has been directed towards their study by criminologists and sociologists. The ostensibly "objective" scholars were very much caught up in the value problems of industrial societies. Public definitions of crime as a social problem led to political pressures on such scholars to provide the answers to the "why" questions about crime and, explicitly or implicitly, to suggest what might be done about the problem. Thus, overt political interest in crime and delinquency created the conditions in which many scholars chose to undertake research to try to provide answers to the questions of public concern; the amount of time, energy and money spent on the investigation of criminal deviance in a society seems to depend on the quality and scale of crime, the reciprocal strength of public concern with the problem and the amount of money available, as well as the interest and natural curiosity of certain kinds of sociologists.

Problems of cross-cultural comparison

The confluence of these influences has resulted in an enormous quantity of sociological writing and research on the subject in the United States and comparatively little elsewhere. Thus, a major problem facing analysts is how far the vast output of American sociologists contributes to the understanding of crime and delinquency in other societies. Can American theories and data make up for the paucity of these in relation to other industrial societies? Asking this question may help us to distinguish between sociological concepts and data that refer to social processes that are common to industrial societies and those that refer to the peculiar substantive characteristics of one society. In fact, the lack of conceptualization and research relating to deviance outside the United States makes it very difficult to draw conclusions about those social phenomena that are common and those that are specific. Nevertheless, the general orienting perspective presented in Chapter 2 attempts to direct attention primarily to such common social processes; in particular, these are the processes by which official definitions—and, therefore, rates of crime and delinquency—emerge from the processes of interaction between the social control mechanisms and some of those individuals who conform to those definitions. The study of the origins, maintenance, and consequences of these processes of definition and control were also seen as integral to the deviance perspective. Similarly, the discussion in Chapter 3 of the formal processes of social control and the ways in which they define, label, and give a specific status to the convicted offender, is also referring to processes common to complex industrial societies. All of them, with slight variations, have developed such public rituals for assigning status to and for punishing convicted offenders. These common processes are considered in more detail in this chapter.

If a concern of the sociologist is to compare similar processes in different societies—to adopt a comparative perspective—the empirical study of these processes in different cultures might suggest the ways in which substantive similarities and differences were related to other features of the respective social structures. Unfortunately, this kind of comparative study has been almost nonexistent in the sphere of social deviance in general and crime and delinquency in particular. It thus becomes rather difficult to fill out the abstract perspective presented in Chapter 2 with reliable comparative data. For this reason, most of the examples given in the subsequent discussion relate either to the United States, where there has been extensive sociological theorizing and research in the area of social deviance,, or to England, where the tradition of investigation has been somewhat different in both quantity and character. While the desirability of ultimately adopting a comparative empirical perspective in sociology should be clear, the difficulties of following this directive currently in the case of social deviance arise from the paucity of reliable comparable empirical investigations.

Sociologists have used a wide variety of concepts for understanding crime and delinquency; similarly, a variety of research methods have been adopted to illustrate some of these concepts and to generate others. Some of the major

theoretical and methodological developments in the sociological analysis of crime will be illustrated in the following
chapter in which the changing sociological stances towards
juvenile delinquency are reviewed. No attempt is made in
this chapter to review the conflicting schools of explanation, but rather a series of complementary concepts and
ideas, drawn from several authors is presented. These
concepts are intended to provide a relatively integrated
approach to the understanding of crime placed within the
wider deviance perspective.

However, the point must be made that the concepts used
and emphasized in any explanation or piece of research
are integral to the nature of the theory proposed and share
its assumptions and limitations. Any theory or perspective
selects only certain things out of the total situation facing
the observer, and what he selects depends on the dominant
orienting concepts of the theory; by extension, what is
selected for intensive scrutiny by the investigator will
influence considerably the kinds of methods of investigation
he uses and, therefore, ultimately the data that arise from
his use of these methods. What this means in practice is that
a variety of commonly used sociological concepts such as
social class, social role, or social structure may be common
to different explanations but may be treated very differently
in terms of both theory and method in these explanations.
In other words, the concepts themselves are given different
meanings in different theoretical perspectives; these differences reflect the major internal divisions within sociology
over the 'correct' perspective to be adopted in analyzing the
social world (Winter, 1966). The concepts used by the
authors whose work is drawn upon in this chapter are derived mainly from the sociological tradition of interpretive
understanding which broadly comprises Max Weber's
verstehen sociology, the symbolic interaction of George
Herbert Mead, and the more recent social phenomenology

of Alfred Schuetz. This should be remembered when this discussion is compared to other interpretations.

Official statistics in sociological interpretation

The sociologist who wishes to understand the patterns of crime in a given society is faced first with the task of trying to obtain as accurate a picture of these patterns as possible —that is, to describe the main parameters of crime and criminality. Unfortunately, even this basic task of description, a clear prerequisite for analysis, is made very difficult, if not impossible, in the study of crime. The obvious source of data, a society's official criminal statistics, cannot be taken as reliable indexes of the amount of quality of illegal behavior in a society; nor can the officially convicted individuals be taken as a representative sample of all those committing criminal offenses. These were two errors of the traditional approaches to studying crime, although many sociologists continue to commit the first one, probably because of the lack of other accessible data. It is worthwhile examining in more detail the limitations of the official criminal statistics, for it is only through recognizing these limitations that we can decide how, if at all, the sociologist can use such statistics. Similarly, an examination of the nature of the statistics illustrates several important features of the way patterns of deviance emerge and are maintained.

By using the criminal law and penal processes to define its subject matter, traditional criminology was placed in the position of limiting its study to those people defined as criminal by a court; its population, therefore, was comprised of officially convicted offenders only. Because it was argued that nobody could be seen as a criminal until he had been so defined by a criminal court, the study of those who had not been officially defined was automatically excluded. The complex processes by which some offenders were officially defined as guilty while others were not were taken as given and were seen as analytically nonproblematic. The result of official law enforcement procedures, reflected in the official statistical indexes of "persons found guilty" and "court disposals," were taken as defining the limits of traditional criminology's subject matter. Similarly, the indexes relating to offenses, especially that of "crimes known to the police" (hereafter referred to as CKP), were taken as more or less reliable and constant samples, or at least as useful approximations of all criminal offenses in society so that, for example, if the CKP showed a steady rise over a number of years, the traditional tendency was to assume that this reflected a real increase in the number of actual crimes committed in the community. There is still a tendency for this to be done by sociologists who acknowledge the limitations of the CKP index but who justify their use of such official data for this purpose by arguing that there is no alternative and that these are the best data we have.

The alternative viewpoint proposed here is that with the possible exception of a very small group of offenses, indexes derived from official data on known criminal offenses and offenders are of very little value as measures of the quantity and quality of crime in a society. This does not mean that the official statistics cannot be used usefully by the sociologist but rather that the use he makes of them will be different to that of traditional criminology. A brief examination of some of the statistics' limitations points both to the kinds of uses to which the sociologist may put them and also to some of the important features of crime in industrial societies. Statistics relating to offenders are dealt with first.

There is one general point that both underpins the deviance perspective and raises the problematic character of the meanings given in our society to the terms *crime* and *criminal*. Put succinctly, we are all criminals; there

are very few members of our society who have not at some
time committed at least one act punishable by a criminal
court, and most of us have committed several such crimes.
There have been several studies by sociologists of self-
reported crimes that show that the vast majority of individuals, when interviewed anonymously, admit to extensive
criminal activity. For example, Wallerstein and Wyle
(1947) in such a study in the United States found that over
90 percent of their adult sample admitted to the commission of a range of offenses for which they could have been
prosecuted. The commission of a range of offenses seems
to be a standard feature of mundane social life in our
society; these offenses range from what may be considered
trivial both in terms of the legal punishments and in public
attitudes, such as many traffic offenses or forms of minor
larceny, to more serious crimes, including various kinds of
violence against the person or more serious forms of theft.
The ubiquitous character of criminal activity is one further
reason for rephrasing the kinds of questions the sociologist
should be asking not only about the official statistics relating
to offenders but also about the phenomenon of crime. If
everybody commits criminal acts, can we meaningfully look
for the "causes" of crime? Should we not rather be asking
why so few people are dealt with by the official mechanisms of social control? If we are all criminal to a degree, do
not the key sociological questions concern the processes by
which a very small group is selected and given the official
public label of criminal and the effects of such processes?
Clearly the social control mechanisms are very highly selective in the legal norms they select for enforcement, in their
disposition of organizational resources for control and in
whom they actually select out for control. A recognition of
the ubiquity both of criminal acts and of criminals (defined
simply in terms of those who have committed illegal acts
and not in terms of the official decisions of a criminal court)

thus raises the importance of the meaning industrial societies attach to the words *crime* and *criminal,* for one of the major effects of the public rituals in which we process selected criminals is to lead the members of the society to redefine radically the character and identity of those selected.

It would seem most useful, then, to view these official statistics that relate to individual criminals as summary indexes of the official selection processes; in other words, any analysis relating to the individual summed up in the official statistics will tell us more about the nature of the selective social control processes than it will about the quantity and quality of crime in the community (Cicourel and Kitsuse, 1963a). If, as I have suggested, crime comprises all those activities that contravene the wide range of criminal laws within a society, the official statistics provide us with various indexes relating to some of these activities. The index that is typically used to provide a guide to trends in the pattern of criminal activity is the annually produced compilation of "Crimes known to the police"; a further index, "crimes cleared up," is set against this and is often used by politicians, the mass media, and the public, as well as the police themselves, as one measure of police efficiency. Both these indexes refer to offenses and must not be confused by the indexes relating to offenders. If data on offenders falls short of providing us with a reliable picture of the community's pattern of criminality, what of the other major statistic relating to offenses, that of the CKP?

There are many difficulties involved in interpreting the official criminal statistics as they are currently published; for example, a major difficulty is the division of offenses, for reasons relating to legal processing, into two groups: felonies (the traditionally more serious offenses) and misdemeanors (the traditionally less serious offenses). A similar distinction is made in English law between indictable (more serious) and nonindictable (less serious) offenses. Although different information is collected about the two groups and there are differences between them in their legal processing, there are no independent principled ways for distinguishing between the two categories; thus, the more serious/ less serious distinction, while historically explicable, often appears arbitrary when detailed comparison is made between apparently similar cases in the two categories. A detailed critique of the current presentation of the official statistics is unnecessary in the present context, but familiarity with some of their more important general limitations is useful.

In considering the value of the CKP index, two kinds of criteria can be used to differentiate the heterogeneous mass of crimes included. First, offenses can be subdivided according to the nature of the victims; three broad categories of offenses can be distinguished in terms of the nature of the victims:

1. Crimes with identifiable victims, including, e.g., most property offenses, all offenses against the person;
2. Crimes without identifiable victims, including mainly consensual crimes and often termed "vice," e.g. abortion, certain homosexual and herterosexual offenses, narcotics offenses, gambling offenses;
3. Crimes against the public order or interest, e.g., certain behaviors considered publicly offensive such as drunkenness, traffic offenses; various kinds of disorderly behavior; tax and customs offenses.

Some types of crime are clearly difficult to classify according to this criterion; for example, some crimes "against the State," such as damage to public property, smuggling or tax offenses, could be placed in either (2) or (3) above. However, these problems of classification are unimportant in this context.

The second criterion for subdivision concerns the ways in which offenses come to be included in the CKP index, and here we encounter the crucial matter of the variability of public values towards offenses. Offenses come to the notice of the police in two ways: They are either reported by a member or members of the public, or they are detected as a result of police initiative and action. The three groups of offenses listed above can thus be analyzed in the most approximate way in terms of, first, their reportability and, second, their detectability. When the approximate reportability and detectability for the three offense groups is examined, it becomes clear that there are gross differences between offenses in terms of these two qualities and that, as a consequence, the CKP index must be seen as possessing a variable and unknown relation to the actual crimes in society.

Nearly all the known crimes with victims are known because they have been reported by somebody and not because they have been detected initially by the police. In general, this group would seem likely to have higher reportability than the other two categories. However, within this category there are likely to be big differences between offenses in reportability. Large-scale property offenses, robbery with violence, homicide, and other major offenses of violence against the person are likely to have high reportability; many minor property offenses, especially those carried out within institutional settings such as shops, schools, and factories, have low reportability. Reportability is likely to change in an unknown way for any given offense over time and between areas; one cannot assume constant reportability for an offense. Detectability is obviously low, for the police have to rely on victims or others notifying them of an alleged offense. Routine police activities are confined to publicly accessible spheres, while many crimes with victims—for example, all property crimes by definition—

occur in private settings inaccessible to the police in their mundane activity (Stinchcombe, 1963).

The second category, crimes without victims, has very low reportability; perhaps the only kind of reportability that is at all important here is the rather distinctive kind of reporting involved the police-informer system. But the fact is that nearly all such crimes known to the police are a result of detection; in other words, they arise out of purposive police activity towards these areas of behavior. This does not mean that they have a high detectability but rather that unless the police went out of their way to detect the few that do appear in the statistics there would be an absence of official data in this sphere. For example, prior to the 1967 Act legalizing abortion in England under certain conditions, the annual average number of cases procuring abortion known to the police during the years 1962–66 was 262, whereas unofficial estimates placed the annual figure at something nearer 100,000. In fact, the number of crimes of this category known to the police invariably almost equals the number of crimes cleared up by the police, which supports the idea that it is direct police action that detects the offense, the offenders, and the evidence at the same time, enabling prosecution to proceed immediately and invariably with success. In the same period, an annual average of 248 cases of procuring abortion were cleared up by the police; between 60 and 70 persons per year were brought to trial for these cases (Home Office, 1967).

The situation is similar with the third category of crimes, those loosely termed "crimes against the public order." Only a small proportion of these are known to the police as a result of public reporting, the vast majority being known through purposive action by the police. As with the second category, clearance figures for this group are almost identical with figures of crimes known to the police. Of course the police only detect a very small minority of those who behave in similar ways; again in the absence of large-scale public reporting of these offenses, the official figures for public order crimes known and cleared up reflect the nature of differential police organization and activity. Low reportability and low detectability are thus a feature of this third category too. With regard to police activity, a useful distinction is made by Reiss and Bordua in seeing police action as "reactive" when dealing with crimes with victims, that is, they react to the victims' protests, while for the other two categories they are mainly "proactive" in that they themselves take the initiative and are responsible for the official crime rates in the second and third categories (Bordua, 1967).

It would seem, then, that it is only within the first group, that official data on a small group of offenses may reflect with any accuracy the patterns of offenses in the community. Even for these carefully selected groups of offenses, the kinds of comparisons that both the sociologist and the public want to make, such as the examination of trends over time, may not be viable because of the unknown influences that changes in public reporting habits, in police organization, and sometimes in the law may have on what gets into the official data.

According to the official criminal statistics for England and Wales and studies of officially convicted offenders, the official picture of crime is one of a criminal population comprised mainly of young working-class males whose criminal activity is concerned chiefly with property, violence, and a wide range of offenses associated with the automobile. The official figures of CKP show a steady rise in numbers since 1956 for the main groups of offenses, with a few exceptions. In fact the proportionate increases have varied considerably between offenses: Property offenses CKP (larceny, breaking and entering) have risen by almost three times in the 12 years from 1956, while the number of offenses of violence has more than trebled; sexual offenses in the same period rose by about a third (Home Office, 1969). The automobile, property, and the person are the focal points of official crime in England and Wales, and these focal points are common to most industrial societies, although the official levels and patterns vary considerably between societies.

Cross-cultural differences are well illustrated in the case of homicide, the official figures for which are likely to be more reliable than most other criminal statistics. Wolfgang and Ferracuti (1967), in presenting the case for a subcultural explanation of violence, provide statistics that show that there are big differences between industrial societies in their homicide rates; among these societies, the United States, with a rate in 1960 of 4.5 homicides per 100,000 of the population, has a much higher rate than Japan (1.9 per 100,000). France (1.7 per 100,000), Italy (1.4 per 100,000), England and Wales (0.6 per 100,000) or the Netherlands (0.3 per 100,000). The fact that the United States has an official homicide rate more than seven times that of England and Wales suggests one of the reasons our main source of theories about and research into crime is the United States. Official rates for property and violence offenses in the United States are also well ahead of those in other industrial countries, although as we have suggested, these are much less reliable than the homicide figures and must be treated only as minimum estimates. However, other kinds of evidence suggest that the scale of property theft is altogether different than that in England. In Manhattan, property theft is so common that many householders and flat occupants find it impossible to insure their belongings against theft.

It seems, then, that while we do get a picture of the patterns of offenses and offenders from the official statistics, the differences in reportability and detectability of offenses and offenders place clear limits on the uses to which such statistics can be put. The use of CKP as a guide to the patterns of crime in society and changes and trends in this statistic over time must be treated with the greatest scepticism.

In fact the problem is confounded when police clearance rates (the proportion of known crimes that the police clear up to their own satisfaction) are examined. Taking the two main groups of property offenses, in England and Wales in 1968 offenses against property with violence had a clearance rate of 36 percent, offenses against property without violence had one of 41 percent, whereas one of the more common offenses of violence against the person, malicious wounding, had a clearance rate of 81 percent (Home Office, 1969). In the United States, the overall clearance rate for crimes known to the police is about 25 percent (Savitz, 1967). Clearly the odds are on the side of the offender. Given this situation, it should be clear that to do as traditional criminology and sociology did in searching for the causes of crime by studying those individuals selected by the social control agencies, obviously a minority of all offenders, was a fundamental error.

It does not follow, however, that because of these limitations the official criminal statistics are of no interest or value to the sociologist but rather that the limitations do require that a different perspective be adopted towards them. First, the statistics provide an indication of the rules that a society, through the interpretations of the enforcers, feels it is important to enforce at any point in time and minimum estimations of deviations from these rules; only a handful of these estimations—for example, for murder—are likely to approximate the actual number of deviations from given rules.

Second, two areas are suggested for investigation: the reporting of offenses by the public and police activity in detection and law enforcement. So far sociologists who have worked in this area, such as Skolnick (1966) and Cicourel (1968), have concentrated almost entirely on studying police activity and have clarified the ways in which features of police organization, their relationships with the community, and their interaction with offenders contribute to the production of official crime rates. Studies of reporting are less developed, and we have only a hazy understanding of differential reporting practices. Relevant work in this area relates typically to reporting of particular offenses or reporting in particular organizational contexts; thus, Mary Owen Cameron (1970), in her study of shoplifting, shows that stores differ enormously in their readiness to report caught offenders to the police. She suggests:

> . . . among department stores, "class" stores generally prefer charges against a smaller proportion of arrested persons than do "mass" stores. . . . Prosecution policy of "mass" stores requires less emphasis on screening. Persons who shoplift in "mass" stores are already somewhat self-selected for lower social class status, and the likelihood of a prominent individual or his wife entering a "not guilty" plea and being found so by the court is therefore not so great as in the "class" stores (pp. 117–18).

Other studies focus on offenses committed by employees at their place of work. Robin (1970), in a study of three large department stores, found that the overall prosecution rate of such offenders was 17 percent but that this covered an enormous variation in prosecution policies between the stores. The respective prosecution rates were 2 percent, 8 percent, and 34 percent. Evidence generally suggests that if the victim is an organization or bureaucracy, the likelihood of prosecution is lowered and at the same time the neutralization of guilt feelings among offenders is facilitated (see Smigel and Ross, 1970, and Martin, 1962). The National Opinion Research Center's study of victimization also provides interesting comparative material on rates of crime as experienced by victims and those reported by the police, on proportions of crime reported to the police, and on reasons for not reporting crime (Ennis, 1967).

Third, while recognizing that statistics relating to convicted offenders should be viewed mainly as indexes of official action, nevertheless, official action may locate areas or neighborhoods in which certain kinds of law-breaking are fairly common and where there are high concentrations of officially known criminals and delinquents. The well established sociological finding that some neighborhoods have high official crime rates while other adjacent and similar neighborhoods have low official crime rates is of interest to the sociologist, and the alternative perspective suggested in Chapter 2 would considerably widen the scope of sociological investigation into such differences. For example, it would be as important to examine the standard police methods of locating suspects as it would be to study the social meanings the officially criminal population attached to their delinquent activities for example, see Sacks, (1972). However, the problems of identifying the unofficial criminals in the "low rate" or the "high rate" areas are likely to be as great for the sociologist as for the police, for obvious reasons. Similarly, the statistics may occasionally provide an unexpected bonus by directing attention to previously ignored phenomena. An example of this would be the recent finding in a study of delinquency in an inner London borough that there were vast differences in the official delinquency rates of overtly similar secondary schools within the borough (Phillipson, 1971).

Fourth, the criminal statistics that relate to the processing of detected offenders that summarize court actions towards offenders—can be useful indexes of trends in official control practices. In other words, consistencies or changes in court practices can be examined, for example, in relation to the changing use of prison, probation, or fining for different groups of offenders.

The article by Christie (1968) suggests how comparative analysis of penal statistics can be used to clarify our understanding of changing penal values. An earlier and more detailed study by Rusche and Kirchheimer (1930) offered a Marxist interpretation of punishment in which the changing use of different kinds of punishment (transportation, galley ships, imprisonment, fines) was seen as determined by economic conditions and especially the market demand for labor. Similarly, if one includes in official materials not just the bare statistics but all the reports and documents that comprise any offender's "official biography" (compiled by police, probation officers, social workers, teachers, and prison and institution officials), an enormous field of research possibilities is opened up. How are these highly selective and truncated reports compiled? How are the stereotypes and labels employed in reports used practically in the disposition of cases (for example, by courts or parole boards)? Does an individual's "identity" as contained in such documents become the controlling identity for officials in their transactions with him? The use to which the researcher puts such materials must be guarded, for as Garfinkel (1967, Ch. 6) succinctly puts it, there are "good organizational reasons" for what, from the researcher's point of view, are "bad clinic records.'" The records are *not* to be treated as accurate diaries or mirror reflections of "what actually happened" in an organization's handling of a client or offender, but they can be used to see how the organization constructs and then utilizes practically an offender's identity.

Finally, the implications of this way of looking at the official statistics for the questions asked by sociologists are radical and relate to the discussion of the normality of

crime in Chapter 3. If crime is a normal phenomenon, if
most members of society commit criminal acts either occasionally or frequently, and if, as the statistics show, many
offenses carry low expectations of conviction, should we
be asking not why is there so much official crime, but why is
there so little? Similarly, should we ask not why those who
did get caught committed their offenses, but rather how
so many people "get away with it" and what are the effects
of not "getting away with it" for the caught offenders and
the community? Once again, these questions take us back
to the relationship between the "law-abiding public," the
official offenders, the unofficial offenders, and the agencies
of social control.

These, then, are some of the limitations and the possibilities of the official descriptive data on crime and criminals.
The first apparent task of the sociologist, that of describing
accurately the quantitative and qualitative dimensions of
crime, is thus seen to be ruled out by the impossibility of
accurately measuring crime in the community; if the descriptive task is not possible, this would seem to call into
question any interpretations or theories of crime causation
that are founded initially on such inadequate data. Clearly,
the sociologist, whatever his theoretical stance, cannot explain or interpret adequately any phenomenon he cannot initially describe. Any such explanations become
either gross distortions of reality or so divorced from
reality that they seem to be vacuous rhetoric directed to
other sociologists. Explanations of both kinds have ap-
peared with disappointing frequency in criminology and
sociology.

Describing Social Process

The alternative perspective at least has the virtue that
the phenomena with which it is concerned are potentially

describable and hence sociologically understandable; they are open to sociological investigation although not necessarily of the conventional kind. Description of certain social processes within which deviance emerges does seem to be possible, and this enables the sociologist to offer an interpretation. In particular, his interpretations are generally directed to showing the relationship between the criminal or deviant phenomena he describes and other social processes that may appear initially to have little to do with deviance. The unconventional can only be understood by seeing how it is inextricably intertwined with the conventional. The rest of this chapter is concerned with the kinds of questions the sociologist might ask in trying to describe and understand criminal deviance; three American sociologists who have made significant contributions to the sociological analysis of deviance—Becker, Matza, and Lemert—provide the main orienting concepts.

Making, breaking, and enforcing rules

Although it may be a truism, there can be no deviance and therefore no crime without rules. Perhaps it is the painfully obvious character of this statement that accounts in part for the almost total refusal of sociologists to take any notice of its implications until very recently. Howard Becker, in *Outsiders* (1963), is the first sociologist to have made explicit some of these implications. In his words:

> . . . social groups create deviance by making the rules whose infraction constitutes deviance, and by applying those rules to particular people and labeling them as outsiders. From this point of view, deviance is *not* a quality of the act the person commits, but rather a consequence of the application by others of rules and sanctions to an 'offender'. The deviant is one to whom that label has successfully been applied; deviant behavior is behavior that people so label (p. 9).

In fact, Becker distinguishes between rule-breaking behavior, by which he means those rule infractions that have
not been successfully sanctioned by society (for example,
the unidentified criminal law-breaker) and deviant behavior, that is, those behaviors that have been labeled and
sanctioned as such by others.

In making this distinction, Becker is suggesting that a
recognition of the process of labeling someone a deviant
following his commission of a given act may be crucial
for an understanding of his subsequent rule-breaking. This
point will be taken up in looking at Lemert's contribution.
However, in drawing attention to the rules which are
created and enforced at the societal level, Becker is pointing
to a sphere previously ignored by most sociologists of
deviance, that of politics. The criminal laws of complex
industrial societies are generated in the political sphere, and
the actual form in which any given law emerges is usually
the result of a long process of argument between conflicting
interest groups. The law resulting from such conflict is
likely to be very much a compromise between the different
interest groups and not necessarily representative of one
particular standpoint. A recent example of such compromise in England would be the Homicide Act of 1957, which
drew the distinction between capital and noncapital murder in an attempt to satisfy both the retentionists and the
abolitionists. Similarly, the Act of 1967, which widened the
conditions in which abortion could be legally performed,
was the result of much bitter disagreement between organized pressure groups such as the Roman Catholic Church,
sections of the medical profession, and the Abortion Law
Reform Association. The resulting law seemed very much
a compromise and open to many different interpretations.
Becker suggests that the rules of a society may reflect the
particular interests of those in a society who are in a position
to create and then to ensure the attempted enforcement of

these rules; these groups or individuals are referred to by Becker as "moral entrepreneurs." The rule creators are, typically, moral crusaders concerned with certain highly valued ends that usually involve translating a general value into a specific rule or law. The specific laws are drawn up by the professionals, typically lawyers, and they are responsible for fitting the new law into the existing web of legislation; they too have values that may enter into the framing of the rule.

Gusfield's (1963) study of the American Temperance Movement and the enforcement of Prohibition documents clearly the rise and demise of a movement of "moral entrepreneurs." His analysis illustrates the contingent character of the production of rules and shows how the analysis of deviance leads inevitably to issues of political power and questions about the access to the means of rule creation and enforcement among different social groups (for a similar study of narcotics legislation, see Duster (1970).

The enforcement of the new rule may require a new body of enforcers, as in the case of factory legislation, or it may be placed in the hands of the existing enforcers, typically the police. To the latter, rule enforcement is a job, and the enforcers initially may have little interest in the actual content of the law; where the enforcers' interests do not center in the content of the rule but rather in the techniques of enforcement, there is considerable latitude for them to develop their own scale of priorities of enforcement. Although these priorities are subject to external pressures from the rule creators, the politicians, the mass media, or the public directly, the discretion of the enforcers is considerable; they thus develop informal rules and methodical techniques for enforcing the formal rules. The official criminal statistics are a result of the consistent application of these informal rules. From Becker's (1963) point of view, then, deviance and those labeled as deviant must be seen as

... a consequence of a process of interaction between people, some of whom in the service of their own interests make and enforce rules which catch others, who in the service of their own interests, have committed acts which are labeled deviant.

By pointing out that the creation of rules is a political act, Becker calls into question the consensual quality of the criminal law and forces us to ask whose interests any given body of law represents. One immediate question would be: Are there any areas of criminal law that would attract universal agreement or consensus. The only certain answer to this is that there is consensus about those laws that have fallen into disuse for a variety of reasons. Empirically there is obviously no consensus because everybody is involved in some kind of rule-breaking intermittently. Yet the problem of consensus can be looked at in another way, and it is a way that suggests Becker may have overdrawn slightly the picture of conflict and disagreement over rule creation and enforcement.

If, as Becker suggests, rules are created and maintained as a result of the processes of pressure group politics, one can examine those areas of the criminal law that continue to be enforced, however selectively, but do not seem to have attracted the attention of a reforming pressure group; two areas stand out as having been largely untouched by such groups: offenses against the person and offenses against private property. There have certainly been and still are reform groups whose concern is to change what is done in the name of society to offenders in both these groups, and changes in the forms of punishment have been effected as a result of their pressures; but any organization that has taken place on the other side of the law in these areas has been directed not at changing the law but at breaking it. Perhaps at this point it is useful to refer back to Mead's analysis that was summarized in the previous chapter. Although he did not specify the crimes to which he was referring, his analysis seems most pertinent in relation to crimes with victims; members of the community, in developing and accepting the ritual public processing and punishing of criminals, symbolically place themselves in the role of the victim and his or her relations. Taking the role of the victim creates a recognition of the identity of interests of self and victim; the self-interests, whether protection of property or body, are similar to those of the victim. This recognition leads to an acceptance of the legitimacy of law and punishment in such areas of behavior; in this case the sociological problem becomes one of understanding how individual offenders neutralize the moral bind of the law in particular situations enabling them to victimize another. The tacit agreement of both the regular rule breakers and rule keepers to the continued enforcement of the laws that outlaw crimes with victims seems to reflect the taken-for-granted belief that the rule-breaker stands to lose as much as the rule keeper by the abolition of these laws.

The processes of rule creation and differential rule enforcement, then, are the background against which any further study of deviance must be set; indeed, the role of moral entrepreneurs in these processes would seem particularly important in relation to the rules creating crimes without victims and crimes against the public order. Becker confines his examples to such crimes, the rules for which seem much more open to changes than crimes with victims. A more detailed discussion of these and other issues concerning crimes without victims is presented by Schur (1965).

It is worth noting, too, that the distinction between rule creation and rule enforcement is never so clear cut in practice as this discussion has implied. Only if we restrict rule creation to the *original* production of the rule as a legal "ideal" in and through the work of political institutions does the distinction hold. In terms of the everyday routine practices of both officials and "lay" members of society the law is being continuously created, re-created, and modified. This is exemplified in the importance of legal precedents in case law as providing the reasoned grounds for current decisions. In other words, it is not the abstract ideals embedded in the formal statute that guide routine enforcement practices, for these contain no recipes for actions or sets of instructions as to how they are to be applied in particular contexts. The application of law (enforcement) in contingent upon the development of routine procedures for "seeing" the abstract letters of the law as "fitting" or "relevant to" a given case.

The other side of law-making is also important in this context; those laws and public orders that define what is to be done to the offender once found guilty not only are a result of and subject to the same sorts of political processes, but they are also closely bound up with the deviance-producing processes in a society. If a society changes the ways in which it decides to deal with certain groups of offenders, the changes will have unintended consequences that will be reflected in subsequent patterns of deviance. The arguments of Erikson and others concerning the effects of penal institutions, together with the rates of recidivism following institutionalization, suggest that any changes in the patterns of use of penal institutions (such as the introduction of the detention center in England following the 1948 Criminal Justice Act) will have unknown effects on the levels of rule-breaking and deviance; in view of the evidence, it seems most unlikely that an increase in either the use of existing institutions or in the creation of new ones will do anything other than increase the amount of rule-breaking in the community. A recent piece of English legislation making fundamental changes in the ways in which our society deals with juvenile and young offenders, the Children and Young Persons Act of 1969, will have an unknown effect on the official figures relating to juvenile delinquency because it changes radically the relationship between the police and the juvenile offender; similarly, the Act proposes major and long-term changes in the pattern of institutions for juvenile offenders that, when developed, will undoubtedly play a considerable, although largely unknowable, part in the dynamics of juvenile deviance. Thus it is not only changes in the criminal law that are important in defining the limits of deviance but also changes in any part of the social control apparatus a society has developed to deal with deviants; many of the organizations explicitly concerned with social welfare may be seen as parts of a society's social control apparatus so that the variety of sources of direct influence on deviance is considerable.

The "ordinary" and "routine" character of most crime

We have seen that in accepting the normality of crime the sociologist's attention is drawn towards issues other than the "causes" of crime; thus, in interpreting the pattern of crime presented in the official statistics, his problem is one of seeing the production of such statistical rates as the outcome of a complex joint enterprise rather than as a reflection of actual crime in the community.

Recent studies describing the routine practices in social control institutions through which "justice" is conventionally accomplished illustrate neatly the gap between our typically unquestioned abstract ideals about what "justice" is and how it works and the everyday means for its accomplishment. Indeed the connection between the abstract legal and philosophical senses of the ideal of justice and the routine work of police and courts is tenuous, to say the least. Analysis of the processes of plea bargaining and the negotiation of guilt show the gap between political ideals and actual practice (see, for example, Blumberg, 1967; Newman, 1962b; and Sudnow, 1965).

The word *normality* also suggests another feature of crime; far from being extraordinary, most officially processed crime is rather ordinary and generates little excitement or interest; it is ordinary in part because it happens all the time. A crime has to be both unusual in its character and relatively rare in its commission to arouse the interest and passions of many members of the society; when they do occur, such crimes are invariably given much attention in the mass media. Ordinary crimes are by and large left to the local press to report selectively.

Focusing on the mundane character of most crime points to a further feature of rule-breaking in our society that was first made explicit by David Matza (1964) in *Delinquency and Drift*. Opposing the traditional positivist perspective that had continually sought but signally failed to demonstrate how different criminals were to the law-abiding members of the community. Matza argued that the key to understanding delinquency was to recognize how closely it was integrated with the surrounding culture. Far from being separate from or the antithesis of "conventional" culture, the culture of delinquency, and by extension much crime, could only be understood by a recognition not of its differences from but of its similarities and integration with the surrounding social world.

We have seen that rule-breaking, including criminal rule-breaking, is very common in our culture; there are few individuals who do not contravene—some of them frequently —rules that are publicly sanctionable. Yet, typically, much of this rule-breaking is not viewed as crime by the actors; for many acts, such as stealing from work, there exists a series of justifications and beliefs that renders application of the term *crime* apparently redundant because the actors themselves and the rule enforcers share the belief that such acts are all right under the circumstances. The meaning of the act changes according to the situation; where there is a reasonable coincidence in the beliefs of the actor, the victim, and the enforcer that a given act is not really a crime (or perhaps that it is not a crime worth bothering about, which amounts in practice to the same thing), then the meaning of the word *crime* itself is called into question. The mutual unspoken agreements to treat given acts as "all right under the circumstances" or only as privately rather than publicly sanctionable, suggests the need for empirical rather than abstract definitions of crime. This means recognizing that the universality of rule-breaking is attended by extensive particularism in the definition of crime through rule enforcement. The breaking of criminal laws seems to be an extension or reflection of the rule-breaking which is a continuing feature of conventional social processes. There is no clear-cut line that can be drawn between rule-breaking of a noncriminal kind and breaking the criminal law.

A further feature of Matza's discussion reinforces the view of integration rather than separation. In looking at the values expresseed in juvenile delinquency, Matza argues that, far from being the antithesis of conventional culture, as many have argued, they seem to be extensions, exaggerations or sometimes badly-timed expressions of quite ordinary values. Excitement, masculinity, and a distaste for mundane work are the values reflected in ordinary male delinquency and are also values shared in common with most male members of society; Matza argues that these are typically regarded as "leisure values" in conventional culture. The surrounding culture, however, expresses these values in somewhat different ways in typically nondelinquent, although often morally marginal, situations.

Again, similarity and not difference expresses the relation-ship between some of the typical juvenile rule-breakers' values and some of those expressed by the surrounding community.

A third feature of ambiguity about rule-breaking in our society can be found in the area defined by E. H. Sutherland (1949) as "white-collar crime;" he was referring to the rule-breaking of those in high-status occupations in the course of their work, although he actually narrowed the field down in his own investigations to the study of offenses committed by business organizations. Governments create many laws to control business activity; these relate to such things as the control of monopoly development, false advertising, various forms of taxation, working conditions and many others. In only a few of these areas is rule-breaking liable to criminal prosecution, as most such activity falls under the aegis of the civil law or administrative regulations of var-ious kinds. Punishments for such rule-breaking are qual-itatively different from those meted out by the criminal courts, usually taking the form of fines or orders to "cease and desist" the particular rule-breaking activity. The strength of government inspection and control is often weak, and the kinds of policing necessary to control ade-quately this kind of activity do not seem to have been attempted by governments in capitalist societies. It is com-paratively easy, therefore, for business organizations to break many of these rules, since their enforcement invari-ably lacks teeth.

In some senses, these offenses are rather similar to crimes against the public order, because the official regulations typically outlaw the activities, as being "against the public interest;" nevertheless, the organizations are processed very differently by the community. The lack of interest of the public in such offenses may stem to a considerable ex-tent from the fact that they are treated so differently; the crucial feature of public stigmatization and the processes of status and identity change inherent in our penal processes are remarkably absent from our kid-glove handling of delinquent business enterprises. Moreover, the values that such activities represent may not be very different from what is actually applauded as "good business" in society. It seems to be very difficult to draw a line between what is defined as good business practice and offenses against the public interest; many such offenses may actually be justified, therefore, as simply minor modifications of the business ethic. But however such infractions are justified by the individuals in the responsible organizations, the differential character of law enforcement and punishment suggests a double standard of law enforcement—one for the individual and one for the organization. They also reflect both the considerable ambivalence and uncertainty in our society about the role of law and punishment and the prevalence of institutionalized rule-breaking. Thus, noting the extensive character of organizational offenses and their acceptance and tolerance by public and enforcement agencies, together with the fact that those responsible are generally regarded as the backbone of conventional culture, reinforces Matza's emphasis on the similarities rather than the differences between criminal rule-breakers and the surrounding culture.

Another feature of rule-breaking in conventional culture that did not directly concern Sutherland but would be relevant to Matza's point and of interest to the sociologist of deviance would be professional malpractice. Occupational groups that attempt to be exclusive by controlling entry to the occupation are expanding rapidly in our society; the older professions, such as medicine and the law, are being joined by newer ones modeling themselves on similar lines. Their work is generally one involving the provision of some services for a client, and the nature of the relationship between the professional and a client can be open to various sorts of exploitation and manipulation; apart from governmental regulation, which is often difficult to invoke if the client does not know his rights, the professions attempt to police themselves.

In a study of the legal profession, Carlin (1966) shows how the social organization of the profession and the social context of lawyers' work effects their ethical behavior. His data suggest that the structural conditions experienced by lawyers at different levels of the professional status ladder provide very different pressures toward and opportunities for malpractice and violation of ethical standards. Thus, the lower the status of the lawyer's clientele and the lower the courts in which he works, the greater are the pressures to violate and the lower are the pressures on him to conform. Moreover, very few violators are caught and punished by the formal disciplinary machinery of the bar; he estimates that only about 2 percent of lawyers who violate generally accepted ethical norms are processed, and fewer than 0.2 percent are officially sanctioned. Such formal controls tend to be invoked only when the offense is publicly visible, and if only some violations are highly visible, few violators need be caught and punished. Care is taken to prevent knowledge of professional malpractice getting outside the profession because of the possible damage to the reputation of the profession. As in the case of mundane criminal offenses, we must presume that the handful of cases of professional malpractice which are publicly dealt with, such as the gross negligence of a doctor in an operation, forms only the tip of a large iceberg of professional rule-breaking. Thus, those professions with the highest prestige and the most developed forms of organization are in the best position to provide immunity from law enforcement for their delinquent members.

Primary and secondary deviance

Having emphasized the common character of rule-breaking, the difficulty of drawing clear lines between criminal and noncriminal activity, and the consequent integration of deviance with conventional culture, the processes through which some deviants are selected and their consequences can now be examined. It is as a result of these processes that any separation that does exist between deviant and conventional worlds seems to arise. The distinction drawn by Lemert (1951) between primary deviation and secondary deviation provides an orientation to these processes.

Lemert proposes that the study of deviation must distinguish between two broad categories of deviation with distinctive etiologies. What he terms "primary deviation" includes the *original* "causes" or reasons for an individual's first deviant acts. These primary reasons for the first deviant acts are likely to be almost as heterogeneous as the situations in which deviance can occur; we have suggested in this chapter that the vast majority of the population intermittently commits criminal acts, and the enormous range of situations in which these acts occur preclude any simple explanations of their origins. Explanations for this range of activity would have to subdivide the field extensively and would require situational analyses of these early rule-breaking acts. Lemert's main point, however, is that these first acts, whether tentative and probing or calculated and unambiguous, are unlikely to have profound effects on the individual's beliefs about himself; the typical response is for the actor to view the initial deviant act as a minor aberration justifiable under the circumstances and bearing little relation to his estimate of the sort of person he "really" is. The act or acts become, in Lemert's words, "merely troublesome adjuncts of normally conceived roles" (Lemert, 1951, p. 75). Lemert refers to the process by which the actor fits the commission of the deviant act into his existing conception of himself as "normalization," which is often supported culturally in a variety of ways. Deviance at this stage is viewed, therefore, as a normal variation of everyday behavior, which has "only marginal implications for the psychic structure of the individual," and the deviations remain primary "as long as they are rationalized or otherwise dealt with as functions of a socially acceptable role" (p. 75).

The limitation of deviations to this stage hinges crucially on the reactions of other people, which may be expressed in varying strengths of moral indignation, and in particular on the reaction of formal social control agencies. The form these reactions take may create moral and practical problems for the deviant actor to resolve; particular problems for the criminal deviant arise from the stigmatization, the punishments, the segregation, and other forms of social control he may experience in response to his primary rule-breaking acts. If the responses of others to the primary deviation effectively differentiate the deviant from his normal milieu, either symbolically or actually, this creates moral problems for him that require resolution. When these problems are resolved, either partially or completely, by subsequent deviation, Lemert classifies them as "secondary deviation." The intensity and formality of society's controlling reactions to deviation and their consequent stigmatizing effect become of central importance for the deviant. The more severe the controlling reaction, the more difficult it becomes for him to normalize his deviation; he is required to reassess its meaning for himself and to undertake some self-reorganization. There seem to be two general directions this reorganization can take: First, the individual may adopt another normal role, either abandoning his deviant actions altogether or finding a more tolerated form of deviance; second, he may move towards the assumption of a deviant role. Lemert says of the second alternative, "When a person begins to employ his deviant behavior or a role based upon it as a means of defense, attack, or adjustment to the overt and covert problems created by the consequent societal reaction to him, his deviation is secondary" (p. 76).

In fact, the full-fledged secondary deviant, the person whose "life and identity are organized around the facts of deviance," is liable to emerge from a progressive sequence of interactions between himself as deviant and the social controllers, in which societal reactions compound the development of the deviant's emerging identity. The secondary deviant is one for whom his deviant status is of primary importance.

Lemert suggests the probable sequential process, comprising a series of stages, out of which the secondary deviant emerges. A similar scheme has been proposed subsequently by Wilkins (1964), who terms it a "deviation-amplification system." Both schema see the individual emerging with a deviant identity out of a progressive sequence of interactions between the deviants and the social controllers. Initial deviance leads to segregation, which leads to more deviance, which leads to more severe punishments, which lead to yet more deviance, and so on, perhaps *ad infinitum*. The deviants, progressively excluded, come to develop identities that center on the deviant status and life styles to match.

The distinction made by Lemert between primary and secondary deviation occurs in a more general discussion of social control in which he also distinguishes between active and passive social control. The latter refers to an aspect of conformity to traditional norms, while active social control is a process for the implementation of goals and values. Active social control is extremely variable in terms both of the values chosen for implementation and of the forms of implementation and is subject to a varieties of pressures. Because of this variability, Lemert argues, it is meaningless to talk in abstract terms about "delinquency," for the activity that becomes known as "delinquent" and those individuals whom we refer to as "delinquents" only arise out of the complex processes of interaction between the active social controllers and selected rule-breakers. It seems clear, he argues, that "'delinquency' in our society has no substantive meaning in a sense of a form or essence of behavior which can be described independently of judgments and symbolically colored reactions of others to it" (Lemert, 1967, p. 25). He therefore proposes that the sociologist study the processes and contexts in which delinquent meanings are attached officially and unofficially to a variety of behaviors, for it is in such processes that deviant identities are assigned and emerge.

The development of a deviant 'career' and 'identity'

Becker provides the final orienting concept for this discussion in his use of the term *career* and the allied notion of personal "commitment" to the career. Career usually refers to an individual's pattern of movement in his occupation, and certain kinds of commitments are prerequisites for "progress" in the career; similarly, there may be typical contingencies or stages in any particular occupational career that are seen as indicators of such progress by those inside and outside the occupation. Becker (1963) argues that the career analogy offers useful insights into the processes of transition from normal to deviant status, the emergence of a deviant identity, and the entry into a deviant group or world. The analogy may have limitations if it is applied indiscriminately to all forms of deviance, as Lemert (1967) has pointed out, but when applied to the sequence of experiences of many delinquents and criminals, it sensitizes us to important features of the emergence and maintenance of deviant identities and groups.

Initially, the contrast might be drawn between those who flirt with delinquency or crime on a casual basis and then drift back into convention and those who follow up their initial flirtation with progressive involvement in crime. For example, a study of juvenile delinquency in East London found that about 50 percent of boys who appear before a juvenile court do not reappear before a court while they are juveniles (Power, 1965); this would seem to be a useful starting point for examining the juvenile careers of selected boys from the two groups. Of obvious importance in this example would be how the juveniles were selected for formal rather than informal action in the first place and the nature of the interaction between them and the social control agencies both at first court appearance and subsequently.

The idea of commitment directs attention to those who continue their rule-breaking activities over a considerable period and who increasingly see themselves as deviant; deviance becomes, if not the main activity around which their life is organized, at least of continuing importance in the way it impinges on other activities and relationships. Becker argues—and there is a good deal of evidence to support this—that typically deviant motives are socially learned in interaction with other rule-breakers; very often subcultures emerge that are either organized around particular kinds of deviant activity or identity, or for whose members certain kinds of deviance are recurrent activities and are comfortably integrated with other group activities. Thus a major concern of sociologists in the field of deviance, in general, and crime and delinquency, in particular, has been in the varying forms of group support for deviant activities. It is obviously not suggested that group support is a necessary condition of either initial or continued individual rule-breaking, but rather that this is a typical concomitant of much deviance, and one that contributes to the building and maintenance of individual deviant identities. In fact, two studies of particular groups of criminals point to the opposite feature, that of isolation from other deviants as being a concomitant of the criminal enterprise: Cressey's (1953) study of embezzlers and Lemert's (1958) study of naive check-forgers both established that these offenses were typically committed in isolation from other criminals. The individual forger or embezzler developed his own justifications for the act. These studies, coupled with the immense variety of possible criminal deviations, suggest that it is certainly possible to undertake both initial and continued deviance without group support, but whether a deviant identity emerges and is sustained depends very much on other people's definition of the rule-breaker. The question of subculture will be considered in more detail in the next chapter in relation to juvenile delinquency.

Like the other writers, Becker gives considerable importance to the contribution of the labeling process to the building up of a deviant identity. The process, discussed by Garfinkel (1956), by which the status degradation of the criminal law-breaker publicly takes place, results in the imputation of a "master status" by others to the deviant. Whereas previously the individual may have been to others, first and foremost, a "reliable clerk," a "lazy husband," or a "quiet neighbor," he is seen after the public ceremony as "after all really a thief." Not only do others now change their behavior towards him, they also typically reinterpret his past biography as leading up to this deviant act "all along;" his past life is examined and clues sought that will "explain" and confirm his deviant character. In other words, retrospectively he is seen as having been "essentially" a thief all the time; his deviant act, viewed retrospectively, is seen as the natural culmination of his "real," "underlying" identity.

This imputation of identity is associated, too, with what Becker calls the generalized symbolic value which a deviant trait or act may be given by others; this is the tendency of others to assume that the actor possesses other undesirable traits they believe are associated with the new label or status. A thief is assumed to possess generalized dishonesty and is certainly viewed as likely to do the same sort of thing again; others may fill out their picture of him by imputing other sorts of personal characteristics to him also. This is the process of stereotyping; from a few isolated biographical details a generalized picture is built up of the individual. Inevitably the stereotype of the deviant is unfavorable, for the "evils" of his particular deviance are commonly held to have been produced by other preceding "evils" in his character. Another area of deviance in which people behave largely on the basis of stereotypes is that of mental disorder; there is a wide variety of labels (such as "nutcase," "loony," "cracked," "off his head," "round the bend") that are symbolically attached to people defined as mentally ill, and the substantive meanings given to such labels may bear little relation to the labeled person's actual behavior. Nevertheless, people typically behave towards the labeled person not on the basis of his actual behavior but in terms of their stereotype of him. Scheff (1966), in his book *Being Mentally Ill,* has an interesting discussion of the conventional stereotypes found in everyday verbal and visual imagery used in relation to mental illness, while Blum (1970) points to the problem of locating the rules we use implicitly to "recognize" mental illness.

In fact, as Goffman (1963), Wilkins (1964), and others have pointed out, in the comparatively anonymous urban settings in which many of our day-to-day contacts with others are of an impersonal nature, we invariably behave towards others on the basis of stereotypes; the others with whom we have fleeting meetings are treated as representatives of categories rather than as individuals. Now, for most of the time, this presents no real problems; some may not enjoy the depersonalization, but at least it facilitates our interaction with others. But when we behave towards deviants in this way, because the generalized symbolic value of our stereotypes typically imputes other "evil" attributes, the implications may be more serious, especially for the deviant himself. As he builds his identity in interaction with others and, as important others behave towards him consistently in terms of the generalized stereotype, so he has to take their imputations constantly into account. As it is central to other people in their dealings with him, so it perforce becomes central for him. In Becker's words: "the deviant identification becomes the controlling one" (Becker, 1963). The difficulties of side-stepping a deviant identity and therefore of discontinuing deviant activity may be considerable under these circumstances. Jean Genet (1964), in his autobiographical *The Thief's Journal*, illustrates this particular aspect in the emergence of his own rather special deviant identity during his stay at the Mettray Reformatory; his responses to others' imputations are vividly described.

> In order to become a colonist, as the children [in the reformatory] were called, I had to force myself. Like most of the little hoodlums, I might spontaneously, without giving thought to them, have performed the many actions which *realize* the *colonist*. I would have known naive joys and sorrows; life would have offered me only trivial thoughts, those which anyone could utter. Mettray, which gratified my amorous taste to the full, always wounded my sensibility. I suffered there. I felt the cruel shame of having my head shaved, of being dressed in unspeakable clothes, of being confined in that vile place; I knew the contempt of the other colonists who

were stronger or more malicious than I. In order to weather my desolation when I withdrew more deeply into myself, I worked out, without meaning to, a rigorous discipline. The mechanism was somewhat as follows (I have used it since): To every charge brought against me, unjust though it be, from the bottom of my heart I shall answer yes. Hardly had I uttered the word—or the phrase signifying it—than I felt within me the need to become what I had been accused of being. I was sixteen years old. The reader has understood: I kept no place in my heart where the feeling of innocence might take shelter. I owned to being the coward, traitor, thief, and fairy they saw in me. An accusation can be made without proof, but it will seem that in order to be found guilty I must have committed the acts which make traitors, thieves, or cowards; but this was not at all the case: Within myself, with a little patience, I discovered, through reflection, adequate reason for being named by these names. And it staggered me to know that I was composed of impurities. I became abject. Little by little I grew used to this state. I openly admit it (pp. 175–76).

A further important stage in the deviant career that reinforces the deviant's self-conception is entry into an organized group of deviants. The deviant group tends to develop an ideology, just as do other professions and occupations, which justify the members' past activities and give them rationales or vocabularies of motive (Mills, 1963b) for continuing their deviance in the future. As well as these justifications, the deviant also finds solutions to the problems of being deviant already worked out for him; others have faced problems of stigmatization, of dealing with the police or with relations, and they provide him with a range of solutions that facilitates his handling of the problems. Clearly, once the individual has thoroughly absorbed the deviant group's view of the world, the barriers to moving away from the group and adopting conventional world views become considerable. Indeed, the incentive for such a move may be low, for the deviant group's ideology and supports must be viewed not simply in negative terms but also in terms of the positive satisfactions and rewards which accrue from membership. It is not the case that individuals maintain such groups only because they have to, but, to a considerable extent, they do so because their rewards are experienced as emotionally satisfying and certainly as more satisfying than the circumstances of the lone, isolated deviant. Similarly, to reiterate Matza's argument, deviant groups, with their apparently distinctive styles, can only be understood in terms not of their separation from the conventional culture but of their integration within it; such groups are completely circumscribed by the conventional culture and owe any identity which they possess to their ongoing relationships with conventional folk.

Sociological analysis of the prison as an example of one extreme type (see Goffman's description of "Total Institutions," 1961) of formal organization has also produced materials that provide different ways for making aspects of the emergence of criminal careers and identities intelligible. Description of the social relationships and culture through which inmate communities are constituted show the distance between the actualities of prison experiences and political assumptions and ideals. Far from reforming and diverting offenders from deviant careers, the institutional experience may serve to confirm the deviant identity of many inmates and provide a context in which entry into the folkways of criminal groups is facilitated. A wide range of material has now been produced that can sensitize us to a variety of issues germane to the production of deviant characters; thus, a series of studies have displayed the forms of inmate power, status, and role relationships (Clemmer, 1958; Schrag, 1954; Sykes, 1958), the values and norms comprising the inmate "social code" and their relationship to those of the criminal subculture (Sykes and Messinger, 1960; Cressey and Irwin, 1964; Irwin, 1970), the differences between the social structures of male and female prisons (Giallombardo, 1966; Ward and Kassebaum, 1965), the importance of ethnicity in the development of relationships in the prison (Minton, 1971; Jackson, 1970; Malcolm X, 1964), some of the similarities and differences between American and European prisons (T. and P. Morris, 1963; Mathiesen, 1965), and the dilemmas and paradoxes faced by officials in interpreting the conflicting demands of their roles (Hazelrigg, 1968). An examination of this material suggests that an analysis of institutional experiences, where these exist, would be central to any reconstruction of the processes through which a deviant identity is grasped. Sartre's brilliant existential analysis of Genet's life and work displays one way in which institutional experiences are incorporated into the reconstruction (Sartre, 1963).

Finally, it is worth reemphasizing that the move back into the conventional world is hindered by the once-for-all character of the deviant status. As Erickson (1962) points out, we have elaborate rituals for giving this status to individuals, but we have nothing comparable for removing it and reinstating them to their conventional civil status. The ex-convict may justifiably feel that he has paid society's price at the end of his prison sentence, but that is not the way society generally, nor the law enforcers themselves, see it; he remains for others a suspect person likely to re-offend, and others' behavior towards him constantly reminds him of this (Matza, 1969).

The career analogy, then, with its associated ideas of commitment and career stages or contingencies, usefully directs our attention to issues that seem relevant to an understanding of the emergence of deviant identities.

Conclusions

In this chapter we have suggested that if the sociologist's task is one of description and interpretation, the scope of traditional criminological and sociological perspectives on crime is both expanded and changed if the interactionist perspective is adopted. At the descriptive stage, the scope is widened by recognizing the inadequacy of official statistics as reliable guides to the patterns of law-breaking in society; the requirement, therefore, is both to describe the variable processes in which the official statistics are constructed and to describe those situations in which some persistent rule-breakers are assured of immunity from enforcement and stigmatization. In both of these cases attention is drawn, first to the processes of interaction between the public, the rule-breakers, and the rule-enforcers and, second, to the typical meanings through which these interaction patterns are sustained. It was suggested that these processes, once described, can be understood by placing them in the wider political context of rule-creation and enforcement. Similarly, the emergence within individuals of deviant identities and their frequent attachment to deviant groups can be understood as a response called out by the alienating and isolating reactions of social audiences to their primary deviations. In the next chapter the sociological analysis of juvenile delinquency is considered to illustrate in more detail the stages in which the sociological perspective has gradually broadened to include the kinds of processes discussed in this chapter.

5

Sociological Interpretations
of
Juvenile Delinquency

Introduction

This chapter tries to draw from the enormous amount of material on juvenile delinquency generated by sociologists some of the main developments in sociological interpretations of the phenomenon. There are two particular dangers in this approach. The first danger is that of imposing a spurious continuity on these interpretations by implying that each was a logical modification of a preceding interpretation; in fact, some of these investigations and interpretations grew out of very different ongoing sociological traditions and might be said to contradict rather than complement or logically modify each other. Thus, while the approach adopted here is broadly a historical one that traces the major changes in conceptualizations of the phenomenon, in fact, there is not a consensus among sociologists about the "right" perspective to adopt. As a result, many sociologists may partially subscribe to each of the following general orientations. The second danger is that in selecting and abstracting only one or two ideas from each main "school" or author, the richness of the particular contribution is lost and, at the same time, what was said may be distorted by pulling it out of context; the only solution to this is for the reader to examine the original contributions for himself. The selection from and criticism of particular works here are inevitably highly particular and done broadly from the standpoint of the interactionist perspective presented earlier; thus all that can be provided is a general orientation to the sociological tradition of delinquency explanation.

The use of the term "juvenile delinquency"

The special meaning of the term *juvenile delinquency* must first be clarified. The word *delinquency* is typically used to refer to juvenile acts that would be crimes if committed by adults; it also includes a range of "status" offenses or acts that can only be committed by juveniles by definition (for example, drinking under age, truancy, driving under age). Various "welfare" cases in which technically no criminal law may have been broken but where the child may be considered beyond control of the parents or in need of care and protection are typically also included in the category of delinquency. "Delinquency," then, is a more inclusive category than "crime," although the range of inclusion varies considerably between societies.

The introduction of a special word to categorize certain juvenile acts has both legal and social policy implications, for the official intention of the label "delinquent" is to suggest that a given act is something less than a crime when committed by a juvenile; industrial societies have thus developed official processes for dealing with officially identified delinquents which are partially separated from the adult processing procedures.

Platt (1969) has a neat account of the historical origins of the official separation between juvenile and adult crime and ways of processing them; he shows how the category "juvenile delinquency" was an outcome of pressure group politics and how the apparently "liberal" intentions of the female reformers in fact produced a system of juvenile justice that was in some ways more repressive than that which it replaced.

In fact, there is no agreement between societies on the age range of juvenile delinquency, and within societies such definitions change over time; in England and Wales the age of criminal responsibility was raised from eight to ten in 1965 and was raised again to 14 in 1969. Thus the proceedings for dealing with children below 14 is civil and not criminal; for those between 14 and 17, the separate juvenile court system is preserved, and they are still officially delinquents; finally, those between 17 and 21, though dealt with by adult courts, are referred to as "young offenders" in an attempt to retain a tenuous distinction between them and adult offenders, and there are some special court sentences available for this group. In the United States the age limits of juvenile court jurisdiction vary widely between states. In 1966 the maximum age for boys was 16 in six states and 17 in nine (President's Commission on Law Enforcement and the Administration of Justice (1967a, App. A, p. 136). Thirty-five states had an upper age limit for boys of 18, and one state held the age of 21. The situation for girls was similar. In addition, in at least one state (California) criminal court judges had discretion to sentence offenders less than 21 years of age under special satutes for "youthful offenders" which, like statutes covering "juveniles," mitigated available penalties.

The terms *juvenile delinquency* and *juvenile delinquent* are thus legal categories whose actual meaning and content vary considerably between societies and within societies, juveniles of the same ages and offenses being dealt with in different ways in different jurisdictions. This poses an insurmountable problem for traditional approaches that are searching for universal "causes" of delinquency, for the

phenomenon to be causally explained differs greatly between cultures. Also, if as has been suggested, the character
of the social control processes contribute to the form and
size of the phenomenon, the relevance of theories generated
in one jurisdiction to the understanding of the phenomenon
in others, where control processes may be very different,
must be questioned.

However, cross-cultural comparisons from the interactionist perspective are informative in enabling us to define which aspects of deviance and control processes are
common to differing cultures and how their relationship to
other social processes, such as socialization, provide for the
emergence of differences in the production and meaning of
deviance. The ubiquitous character of deviance (see Chapter 3) points to the common processes to be analyzed, while
the substantively different forms deviance and its control
taken in even similar countries (for example, narcotic addiction or organized crime as criminal problems in the
United States and England) show the value of a comparative perspective.

The sociological interest
in juvenile offenders

Before looking at some of the main contributions to the
sociological tradition, a preliminary issue must be raised
briefly: Why has such a large proportion of the work of
those sociologists who have specialized in the study of
crime been concerned with the study of the juvenile? The
answers reflect both the particular social and political
concerns of industrial societies and the particular personal
values and interests of the investigating sociologists. There
has been a marked change in these societies' attitudes towards children and the role of the state in relation to them
since the middle of the nineteenth century. In the specific

case of law-breaking, the change has been from simple punishment and equality before the law with adults to a recognition of children's welfare needs and the state's responsibility to meet these. Officially then, punishment of law-breaking children is supposed to be moderated by a consideration of individual welfare. In effect, being a juvenile in the eyes of the law is an extra mitigating circumstance to be taken into account in the disposition of the case. A further reason is the belief that subsequent criminality stems from early involvement in delinquency, so that if prevention of future criminality is a concern, then the "root" of the problem, juvenile delinquency, should be investigated; certainly a proportion, about half in most studies, of official adult offenders have also been officially identified as juvenile delinquents, but we have little knowledge of the nature of the career transition from official juvenile offender to official adult offender. In fact, the official statistics themselves provide the main clue to this major social and sociological preoccupation with the juvenile offender, for these show that officially the peak age for indictable offenses in England and Wales was 14 for a long period (between the raising of the school-leaving age from 14 to 15, just after the war, to the recent reclassification of a group of nonindictable offenses popular among adolescents as indictable); thus, the early teens provide the period of greatest official risk. However, Power (1962) has shown that if nonindictable offenses (many of which are equally as "serious" as the indictable offenses committed by juveniles) are added to the indictable, the official peak age is more likely to be about 18 or 19. Thus, even society's reliance on the official statistics is found to be somewhat misguided when the full range of offenses are taken into account.

In the United States a similar picture emerges from analysis of the official statistics, for youth is disproportionately responsible for officially handled offenses. This can be seen both from arrest rates in general and from arrest rates for particular offenses. Thus, of all persons arrested in 1965, about 30 percent were under 21 years of age, and about 20 percent were under 18 years of age (President's Commission on Law Enforcement and the Administration of Justice, 1967b, pp. 55–56). The arrest rate for serious property crime (burglary, larceny, motor vehicle theft) shows that the 11-to-17-year-old age group (13.2 percent of the population) accounted for half of the arrests for these offenses in 1965, although obviously not all of the acts included within the legal categories were equally serious (for example, larceny includes thefts of less than $50). An older age group, the 18-to-24-year-old group (10.2 percent of the population), had the highest arrest rate for crimes of violence. This group accounted for 26.4 percent of arrests for willful homicide, 44.6 percent of arrests for rape, 39.5 percent of arrests for robbery, and 26.5 percent of arrests for aggravated assault. However, if juvenile arrests are looked at as a whole, juveniles are most frequently arrested not for the most serious offenses but for petty larceny; fighting; disorderly conduct; liquor-related offenses; and conduct not in violation of the criminal law, such as curfew violation, truancy, incorrigibility, or running away from home. Late childhood and adolescence are thus seen to be the years of greatest risk of being caught for law-breaking, and this has resulted in considerable pressure on criminologists and sociologists to investigate this as a distinct problem.

Finally, in terms of the sociologist's own concerns and apart from any political pressure he may experience or personal interest he may have in the issue of delinquency, at the practical level of research the juvenile delinquent is likely to be defined as a much easier object to study than his adult counterpart; the juvenile is more visible, accessible, gullible, less able to say no, and subject to wider official control than the adult. Moreover, his law-breaking is typically more mundane and trivial so that the consequences of his confiding in an outsider, such as a sociologist, are likely to be defined by him as less serious than would be the case with the adult offender. Of course, none of this necessarily means that the data sociologists obtain from juveniles are any more (or less) reliable than those obtained from adults; that is something that can be decided not in the abstract but only in the investigation of the methodology of each study. Convenience is therefore an added reason for sociologist's concentration on juvenile offenders.

With the exception of the last point, and then only in part, the reasons given for sociologists' extensive concentration on juvenile offenders stem not from sociological values or problems but from the definition of juvenile delinquency as a social and political problem. Through political processes particular groups in society can influence heavily what sociologists study; this brings us back to the points made in the first chapter concerning the value problems of traditional criminology. Exactly the same problem has dogged much sociological investigation of crime and delinquency and has resulted frequently in a blinded approach to the selection of issues and processes for study. The metaphorical blinders worn by many sociologists in their investigation of delinquency were a result, to a considerable extent, of the fact that the sociologists themselves took for granted and shared the society's definition of the problem. Thus many of their explanations seemed to be offered up in response to such political concerns as the "causes" of delinquency and means of eradicating these, and ways of changing those officially found guilty. Few sociologists, until recently, recognized that their asking and trying to answer these questions were simply tying them to the political status quo and obscuring the investigation of more fundamental issues posed in the interactionist perspective.

It was noted in the last chapter that the main official parameters of crime derived from the official statistics focus attention on young working-class males who, usually in small groups, indulge in a wide range of property offenses, minor forms of violence, and more recently, offenses connected with the automobile; basically it is this combination of parameters for which sociologists have offered a variety of interpretations, the main themes of which are now considered.

Sociological interpretation and historical continuity

Most sociological interpretations of delinquency and crime lack a sense of history; those that attempt to account for the origins and emergence of typical patterns of delinquency, for example, some subcultural explanations, rarely attempt to locate such origins in time and place. Similarly, those explanations focusing on the processes of transmission of delinquent values, such as Sutherland's theory of differential association (Sutherland and Cressey, 1960), claim to be concerned with processes that are universally present irrespective of time and place so that history is not a direct concern. The kinds of explanations proposed by sociologists tend to be either classificatory or processual. The classificatory approaches usually provide a set of concepts that are used to classify the actual content and forms of delinquent behavior; such classification schemes are not equipped to deal with historical processes, and only rarely is the historical dimension of the emergence and changes in form and content of delinquency dealt with by sociologists in their discussions accompanying their classification schemes. The most obvious example of such a scheme would be Merton's (1963) paradigm for understanding the relationships between patterns of deviant behavior and certain features of the social structure. In fact, this kind of classification scheme attempts to account for contemporary patterns of delinquency by looking at the contemporary social structure. However, the processual approaches, like differential association, would claim that history is not important for them because their concern is not with particular behaviors but with general processes that are present irrespective of the particular form they may take. Contemporary rather than historical examples are used to illustrate these universal processes for obvious methodological reasons.

This ahistorical character of sociological interpretations of delinquency is a serious shortcoming because these interpretations invariably rest on taken-for-granted assumptions concerning the history of particular societies or communities. A feature common to most interpretations is their attempt to relate particular patterns of individual or group delinquencies to aspects of the social structure. The sociologist has generally tried to show how the overall social position of groups, measured in terms of such things as social class, social status, or educational attainments, provides the background conditions for the emergence and persistence of shared values among those sharing similar social structural positions. In the study of delinquency, this typically meant focusing on the community or neighborhood in which official delinquents were most frequently found and examining selected aspects of neighborhood life considered relevant to the understanding of delinquency; the communities typically studied were those occupying the inner areas of large cities, for it is these in which the highest official crime rates most frequently occur. Explanations offered for patterns of delinquency in such areas, with a few exceptions, fail to account for or often even to consider the sheer historical continuity and persistency of the official patterns. A major problem facing sociological interpretation of delinquency is the fact that many of the areas that are officially defined as high delinquency areas were high delinquency areas more than a hundred years ago and have consistently maintained their official rates throughout the past century.

Data from several sources clearly illustrates this continuity; Tobias (1967) provides a valuable analysis of the official patterns of crime in England in the nineteenth century using both official statistics and a wide array of documentary sources from the period. The so-called criminal class grew out of and was largely maintained by the recruitment of often vagrant but skilled juveniles who were trained and frequently kept by adults for their thieving capacities. As is clear from Mayhew's (1862) vivid descriptions, the "rookeries" in which such juveniles and criminals abounded were often those areas that continued to have high official delinquency rates a hundred or so years later. Mayhew, himself no mean classificatory criminologist, distinguished three main types of young felons who emerged from the mass of younger juvenile thieves: common thieves, expert pickpockets, and burglars. One might add to Mayhew's actual observations the fictionalized account of Morrison (1896) in *A Child of the Jago,* written more than 40 years after Mayhew's work. The Jago, "for one hundred years the blackest pit in London," was a notorious web of streets that, although long demolished and replaced by different streets and housing, nevertheless has maintained consistently high official delinquency rates since the time of Morrison's writing. This problem of historical continuity will be considered subsequently in relation to specific theories.

In looking at the historical roots of the sociological interpretation of delinquency, there were several other nineteenth century writers and researchers whose work provides a background against which to set more recent contributions. The statistical analyses of the continental writers Guerry and Quetelet were the first attempts to relate the official crime statistics to a range of population and geographical indices. At about the same time as Mayhew in England, a German, Avé-Lallement, although not specifically concerned with juvenile delinquency proposed a sophisticated thesis to account for the growth and persistence of criminal groups with their own argot and traditions; he saw such groups gradually emerging from the widespread vagrancy that followed the breakup of the old feudal order. He argued that these vagrant groups, which lived by petty crime and from the proceeds of almsgiving, were forced to change their habits with the rapid growth of cities in the eighteenth and nineteenth centuries and the concomitant development of organized police systems. They were increasingly pushed back into the social order by these new social controllers and were forced to operate by stealth in the relative anonymity of the new cities (Lindesmith and Levin, 1937). Mayhew also had suggested the importance of the urban vagrants as a major source of recruitment to the "criminal class" of the nineteenth century. Here, then, was perhaps the first attempt to account for patterns of crime as a direct product of features of the social structure; it is this kind of general all-embracing theory of crime that is echoed in several more recent contributions.

For many years following these early contributions, the main interest of those investigators of a sociological inclination was in the relationship between crime and delinquency and economic conditions, the general standpoint of such authors being the thesis that poverty was a main "cause" of criminality. These studies, based almost entirely on the analysis of official criminal statistics and their relationship to a series of socioeconomic indexes, were inconclusive and often contradictory. Vold (1958) provides a useful sum-

mary of their findings and some of the difficulties of interpreting them.

The "Chicago School"

However, it was not until the 1920s and 1930s that any
significant developments occurred in the study of delinquency. They grew out of a small-scale revolution in sociological ideas and methods that took place at the University of Chicago. The city of Chicago was viewed as a natural
laboratory for sociological research by the outstanding sociologists who worked there, and a remarkable series of
studies was carried through into a wide range of subjects.
Although the subjects chosen for study often reflected the
major social and political concerns of the period, especially
those arising out of city life and the successive waves of
immigration experienced in America, they also reflected
the natural personal and increasingly sociological curiosity
of the particular investigators with the less respectable
aspects of city life. The main instigator of this upsurge of
research activity was Robert Park; at the same time George
Herbert Mead (1934), also at Chicago, was laying the theoretical foundations of one of the main traditions in sociology, symbolic interactionism. Crime and, in particular,
juvenile delinquency were interests of several Chicago
sociologists; these interests were reflected in a two-pronged
approach to the investigation and explanation of delinquency in Chicago.

The first style of investigation was an attempt to apply
the social ecological theories of Park (1925) to the study
of delinquency. Drawing on ecological ideas from biology
and zoology which emphasized the mutual interdependence
of plant and animal species in a given area, their conflicting
but coordinated interests and the processes of competition,
dominance, and succession among different species, Park

analyzed the social organization of the city, using the same concepts. It was seen as comprising a series of natural social areas that emerged during the processes of city growth and economic development and were particularly contingent on the process of competition for control of the city's natural resources. Park saw the modern city as comprising five main natural areas that formed a series of concentric zones around the city center; each zone had distinctive social and physical characteristics. An important feature of the social ecological approach was to view the social relationships and typical behaviors persisting among those who inhabited each zone as natural social relationships and responses that emerged from the environmental conditions of the zone. These ideas were originally applied to the phenomenon of delinquency by Shaw and McKay (1942), first in Chicago and subsequently in a large number of other American cities. Relating official statistics on delinquency to census population data, Shaw and McKay computed official delinquency rates by census tract for the whole of the city over a period of almost 30 years. They found gross and consistent differences in the rates between the five zones defined by Park; the rates declined proportionately with distance from the city center, and the highest rates were mostly found in the "interstitial" zone which surrounded the city center. This zone, the city's "twilight" area, was characterized by high population mobility, poor housing, and overcrowding and was increasingly corroded by industry; in its social-class composition it was almost completely working class. This pattern of delinquency distribution was more or less reproduced in later ecological studies of other cities. In line with Park's thesis, these high delinquency areas were viewed as natural areas, the delinquency of the boys being seen as largely a normal response to the social and natural characteristics of these communities.

In spite of the natural and normal character of most delin-

quency when seen as a response to environmental characteristics, the main orienting concept used by sociologists of
the Chicago School to understand social and urban problems like delinquency was that of "social disorganization;"
the ecologists and others tended to view the emergence of
high delinquency rates in a community as one indicator of
the social disorganization of that community. Louis Wirth
(1964) and W. I. Thomas (1966) were two of the Chicago
sociologists who used this concept to account for a range of
social problems, and Burgess (1942), a collaborator of
Park's, later went on to apply the concept to Shaw and
McKay's findings. Thomas defined social disorganization as
"a decrease of the influence of existing social rules of behavior upon individual members of the group."

Now, as C. Wright Mills (1963a) pointed out many years
ago, this concept has unfortunate implications that render
its value in sociological analysis questionable. There are
two main problems in using it, one a value problem and
the other an empirical problem. First, if a social situation
is defined by the observer as disorganized, it can only be
disorganized in relation to a given set of principles of organization; but what happened all too frequently when this
term was used was that the principles of organization were
assumed or taken for granted and were not spelled out by
the observer; invariably it turned out that the principles of
organization used as a yardstick for disorganization were
the observer's own implicit, usually conventionally middle-
class, values concerning what *ought* to be. Thus his own
values entered directly into his diagnosis of social disorganization. Second, a situation that is defined as disorganized denies the presence of any typical features of organized relationships. Empirically this is untenable, for the
very behaviors taken as indicators of disorganization actually require a high degree of social organization; delinquency and crime are social activities requiring coopera-

tion, trust, and persistence of relationships if they are to be even minimally successful. The concept of social disorganization, used to diagnose social problems, therefore misleads because it draws attention away from the very features of social relationships through which delinquency and other such phenomena persist. The Chicago sociologists were unable to see the implications of the concept; organization was certainly present in high delinquency areas, but it was not of the form that fitted in with their conceptions of 'appropriate' organization.

One possible use of the concept of social disorganization that seems less open to the above criticisms is in cross-cultural comparisons. It may be possible to distinguish different levels of social disorganization between societies; thus societies in states of civil war, where there may be several warring factions or where there is a dissensus about the appropriate form of central government, may be disorganized relative both to their history and to other societies with similar economic and social structures but without such conflicts. Clearly, within such a 'disorganized' society the various factions and interest groups could be highly organized; obvious contemporary examples would be Vietnam and Cambodia. Between societies it may be possible to distinguish levels of disorganization according to indexes of major internal conflict and instability of previously institutionalized relationships. Such a comparison does not deny the presence of highly organized groups within such a society and takes as its norm of organization either other similar societies or the same society in an earlier period rather than the investigator's implicit personal values. This use of the term comes close in meaning to the concept of anomie, which will be briefly discussed later.

The main contribution of the ecological branch of the Chicago school was thus to emphasize the normality of delinquency in certain neighborhoods and to point to the importance of local community characteristics as providing a natural setting in which delinquent values emerged and persisted. Shaw and McKay had also established that over 80 percent of the official delinquents committed their delinquencies in the company of a few other boys of about the same age; delinquency was very much a group enterprise. It was the study of these delinquent peer groups and gangs that formed the second major contribution of the Chicago school to the analysis of delinquency. Two works in particular are outstanding in their contribution both to the substantive field of delinquency research and to the methodological tradition of general sociology: *The Gang* by F. M. Thrasher (1927) and *Street Corner Society* by W. F. Whyte (1966).

These two studies complement each other, being substantively very different, and also, when taken together, the work of Shaw and McKay. Thrasher, in his mammoth study of over 1,300 boys' gangs in Chicago during the 1920's, traced the typical careers of these groups, showing how the spontaneous play groups of early childhood developed into the highly structured adolescent gangs with their own traditions, argot, sense of loyalty, and control of a 'territory.' Conflict was a central concern of the typical gang, and of particular interest in terms of the deviance perspective was Thrasher's suggestion that gangs increasingly cohered around the values of conflict and aggression as a response to the various attempts by adults and other adolescent groups to control forcibly their activities. Thrasher argued that gangs that indulged intermittently in delinquencies flourished both because they met the common individual needs of belonging and protection and also because the environment facilitated delinquency in a variety of ways, such as the collusion of adults in delinquent activities and weak family controls.

Whyte's study was of a very different kind, being an ac-

count of one particular group of young men, the Norton
Street Gang, whose company Whyte shared for three years.
Although not specifically concerned with delinquency and
crime and although the members of the group were young
men rather than juveniles, several of Whyte's findings
pointed to aspects of the dynamics of group life that are held
to be relevant to an understanding of delinquent peer
groups and have been followed up by subsequent delinquency researchers. First, at a general level, Whyte's study
of this group and its position in the local social structure in
an explicit refutation of the social disorganization approach.
Two other features of his study are important: his distinction between 'corner boys' and 'college boys' posed a
problem for subsequent research which has yet to be resolved satisfactorily. He found that in this socioeconom-
ically homogeneous slum, two distinct responses emerged
among adolescents. A minority attempted to achieve social
mobility by a conscious commitment to middle-class or
college values, with the eventual hope of moving out of
'Cornerville.' There was an early and almost complete split
between them and the 'corner boys.' Two distinctive, mutually exclusive styles of life emerged among adolescents; it
was impossible to be a 'college boy' and still run with the
'corner boys.' In Whyte's own words:

> Both the college boy and the corner boy want to get ahead.
> The difference between them is that the college boy either
> does not tie himself to a group of close friends or else is
> willing to sacrifice his friendship with those who do not ad-
> vance as fast as he does. The corner boy is tied to his group
> by a network of reciprocal obligations from which he is either
> unwilling or unable to break away (p. 107).

The roots of this differential response to the slum situation
have yet to be clarified by sociologists. Finally, Whyte's
analysis of the intra-group relationships, and especially his

emphasis on the importance of the leader in influencing and controlling the group's activities, pointed to areas of analysis that were picked up and elaborated by later sub-cultural theorists. Whyte's study is the classic piece of par-tipant observational research in sociology.

Sutherland's thesis

The theory of differential association proposed by E. H. Sutherland and intended as an all-embracing explanation of the process of learning to become a criminal can be seen as an attempt to marry the two levels of analysis found in the Chicago school's studies (Sutherland and Cressey. 1960). Sutherland hypothesized that a person becomes a criminal or a delinquent when he experiences an excess of definitions encouraging law violation over definitions encouraging law-abiding behavior; these definitions are mediated to the individual largely within intimate per-sonal groups such as the peer group or the family. Suther-land's use of the term *definitions* is really a shorthand version of the concept *definition of the situation* and is derived from the writing of W. I. Thomas (1966); in the context of the theory of differential association, Sutherland was referring to the extent both of one's association with others whose definitions of some situations encouraged the breaking of particular laws and also of one's isolation from others whose definitions of the same situations discouraged the breaking of these laws. The associations an individual has with pro-criminal values and behavior—the nature of his exposure to them—can vary in frequency, duration, priority, and intensity.

Unfortunately the theory as it stands is untestable, for it requires some sort of total accounting method in which an individual's life experiences of definitions favorable and unfavorable to law violation are balanced against each other; the impossiblity of devising such a method in social research will be clear. Nevertheless, Sutherland's theory, despite being empirically problematic, did serve to direct sociologists' attention to the processes of interaction within face-to-face groups; these processes were present in both those neighborhoods with high and those with low delinquency rates. It would follow from Sutherland's thesis that the association of juveniles with pro-criminal and anti-criminal values would be very different in the two neighborhoods; for Sutherland, this differential association comprised the process of becoming delinquent. It seemed to be this theory, taken in conjunction with Merton's discussion of anomie that provided the impetus for the emergence of the subcultural approach to the explanation of delinquency during the 1950s.

Anomie and deviance

Merton's essay was an attempt to clarify and extend the meaning of *anomie*, a term introduced into sociology by Durkheim (1951, 1965). He had used the term to describe extreme situations of normlessness, that is, situations where no clear-cut guides for behavior existed and where previous solutions to everyday problems of living were rendered inappropriate by sudden changes in the social structure; examples of the kind of situation envisaged by Durkheim would be a sudden drastic economic crisis or an unexpected invasion by a foreign power. In situations such as these, the firmly held values and expectations of many sections of the population are called dramatically into question and are rendered irrelevant to the problems faced. Merton's (1963) use of the term, however, differs sharply from Durkheim's.

A main concern of Merton was to account for the differential societal distribution of rates of various kinds of deviant behavior. He argued that societies can be analyzed in terms of the dominant goals all members are encouraged to seek and the legitimate or socially approved ways of achieving these goals. What he called an 'acute disjunction' between the goals and the means for large sections of the population results in strong pressures to deviate from the approved norms. He defined this disjunction as *anomie*. The prime example he took was contemporary American society, in which, he argued, the dominant goals to which all are encouraged to strive is material success through occupational mobility; however, such success is available through legitimate occupational channels for only a minority of the population. Those most unlikely to succeed are the bottom echelons of the social-class hierarchy, and it is among such groups that the acute disjunction or anomie is likely to be experienced most vividly; the pressure to deviate is therefore at its strongest among the most economically and socially disadvantaged groups. As a result, many decide to deviate from legitimate norms in order to achieve the material rewards, and they develop their own means for achieving the goals. He calls this the response of 'innovation' to the situation of anomie. There are other adaptations to these pressures, and he calls these variously 'conformity,' 'retreatism,' 'ritualism,' and 'rebellion.' However, the important response in the present context is that of innovation, for the characteristic innovation, he argues, is property theft; he thus accounts for the high official rates for property offenses among lower working-class groups as an adaptation to the structural strain induced by the disjunction between the goal of material success and the lack of legitimate means for its achievement.

It is unnecessary here to provide an extensive critique of Merton's theory, for this has been done by several authors, notably Lemert (see Clinard, 1964). However, in terms of the interaction perspective, it is worth noting the following points. The theory accepts the official rates of deviance as actually reflecting the real phenomenon to be explained; the distinction between goals and means is tenuous and artificial; the assumption that everybody shares the same basic goal is a simplification and distortion of the complexities involved in analyzing people's life goals; no account is taken of the problematic processes of social control; the model is static and suggests no hypotheses about interaction, for example, in relation to the movement into and out of deviant careers; within the situation of acute disjunction it does not account for differential responses to strain, that is, why in a situation of anomie some conform, some innovate, some retreat, and so on; finally, by focusing on the structural level, it plays down the importance of typical social meanings as they enter into individuals' interpretations of their situations by implying that these meanings are merely products of external social forces. Merton's model, nevertheless, when taken in conjunction with the earlier work on delinquency and peer-group processes of Shaw and McKay, Thrasher, Whyte, Sutherland, and others, provided the basis for the subcultural approach to understanding delinquency.

Sub-cultural interpretations

The concept of subculture is an attempt to deal analytically with the apparent fact that a range of small "societies," characterized by some values that seemingly conflict with or differ from those of conventional society and are contained within the political unit of the total society. Industrial societies are differentiated into a variety of strata or groups, each possessing some distinctive values and behavior patterns. These "societies" contained within the larger one are referred to generally as "sub-cultures." The central problem in the use of the term for understanding the social action of any particular group is: Where does the general culture end and the subculture begin? Are there values that are common to all members of a culture? If so, what are they and how can one differentiate them from the values that are said to be peculiar to particular subcultures?

There have been two useful attempts to relate the discussion of specifically delinquent or criminal subcultures to the more general use of the term in sociology by Downes (1966) in his review of delinquent subcultural theory and by Wolfgang and Ferracuti (1967) in their essay on violent subcultures. Both these discussions lie within the traditional sociological framework; they therefore largely ignore the kinds of issues and criticisms just leveled at Merton's anomie theory and which are also largely applicable to subculture theory. However, their discussions do illustrate clearly the difficulties of using the term *subculture* even when it is used within a traditional framework. Both show that except in a very few cases it is difficult analytically to distinguish subcultural from general values and that in traditional methodology we have few reliable techniques for measuring values even when we can distinguish them. Both seem to agree that the concept can be used most usefully in relation to those groups in which some of their activities run directly counter to values assumed to characterize clearly the general or politically potent culture. The responses of these groups to some of the situations they face are described by Downes as negative responses to the social and cultural structures and can be seen in the actions of delinquent or politically extremist groups; in similar terms, Wolfgang and Ferracuti see the actions of such groups as reflecting untolerated discordant values. Unfortunately, when the difficulties of using the concept which are raised by Downes (1966) and Wolfgang and Ferracuti (1967) are taken together with those criticisms that arise from the deviance perspective, already outlined in relation to the anomie theory, then the concept seems to have serious shortcomings if it is used on its own as a main explanatory device. Some of these shortcomings are illustrated in the main contributions to delinquent subculture theory. The disagreement between the writers is one basic problem of the utility of the concept.

The first of a series of attempts to understand gang delinquency in subcultural terms was that of Cohen (1955) in his book *Delinquent Boys*. Starting from Merton's anomie scheme, he argued that the innovation adaptation failed to account for the distinctive content of the delinquency of working-class boys' gangs. Far from being an attempt to achieve material success through rationally calculated property theft, much delinquency was non-utilitarian and negativistic in character; a great deal of juvenile theft was not done to, and could not, provide the thieves with an illicit income. Nor could the vandalism, damage to property, conflict activities and fleeting escapades with automobiles be construed as attempts to achieve material success by illegitimate means. In fact, Cohen argues, these delinquent activities frequently seemed to be a direct denial of the essentially middle-class values of getting ahead by hard work and material acquisition. This led him to propose a theory of "reaction formation." He hypothesized that working-class boys, like others, share a common problem of status, of gaining recognition and acceptance in the community; however, the boys are ill-prepared by their home and social environment to perform effectively in terms of the conventional criteria of status. These criteria, mediated largely by the school and by other representatives of the politically dominant culture, consist of things such as academic achievement and ambition, good manners, ability to postpone gratification, respect for property, ability to control aggression, and constructive use of leisure;

they comprise the "middle-class measuring rod" by which the boys' performances are measured and rewarded. Because many working-class boys perform inadequately in terms of these criteria, as is constantly made clear to them in school, they are forced to create their own criteria for status and reward. Cohen argues that the boys set up their own criteria by turning upside down the middle-class measuring rod and giving status for those activities that are the very antithesis of its components. Many of their own criteria lead directly to delinquent activities. It is this turning upside down of middle-class values, to recoup some of the esteem denied to them by the conventional culture, which is the core of Cohen's explanation for the emergence of the distinctive content of juvenile delinquency and, therefore, of the delinquent subculture.

Two other contributors to the subcultural tradition provide contrasting accounts of the delinquent subculture. Cloward and Ohlin (1960), in proposing a typology of subcultures to account for distinct styles of delinquency that they claim characterize different neighborhoods, directly modify Merton's theory. They argue that Merton only talked about the availability of legitimate means for achieving material success and ignored illegitimate means. They argue that all youths internalize middle-class success goals at an early age, but in most working-class neighborhoods legitimate avenues for mobility and success are largely closed; however, there may be clear channels for mobility in organized criminal rackets and professional crime. Where these illegitimate means for success are present, the type of delinquency they suggest is very different from that in neighborhoods where adult criminality is unorganized and small-scale. In the first, delinquency tends to reflect and be continuous with adult criminality, being rationally organized for material gain; in the second, delinquency tends to be characterized by the concerns of adolescence in a loosely controlled environment centering particularly on aggression of various kinds against other people and property. Finally, there is a third subculture comprising the "double-failures" and dropouts who, in response to their failure both in legitimate and illegitimate enterprises, take to various kinds of escapist activity, especially hard drug use. These three juvenile subcultures —criminal, conflict, and retreatist—thus arise as a response to the particular pressures and opportunities of their immediate environment.

A third contribution is that of Miller (1958). Working in an anthropological rather than a sociological tradition. Miller emphasizes different aspects of the delinquent subculture in his analysis. He sees a clear split between middle-class culture and the culture of the group at the bottom of the American working class; the two cultures are viewed as quite autonomous, with their own traditions and life-styles. There is little room for overlap or penetration of one culture by the other in Miller's explanation. The culture of the lower working-class is characterized by six "focal concerns:" trouble, toughness, smartness, excitement, fate, and autonomy. These concerns are issues that constantly require the attention of the members of the cultures in a variety of common situations and attachment to the concerns can lead to delinquency in various ways. The origins of these concerns are related to the gradual bedding down of the American class structure following the successive waves of immigration; the bottom section consists of Negroes and the hard core of families of unsuccessful immigrants. Miller argues that the distinctive family structure and relationships that characterize this bottom stratum, especially the female-based household and single-sex peer groups, contribute to and reinforce the delinquency producing aspects of the focal concerns. He thus sees the total social structure comprising at least two distinctive class styles that are culturally discontinuous, one of which generates delinquency as part of its very nature.

There are other contributions to the tradition of delinquent subcultural theory (for example, Yablonsky, 1967), but these suffice to illustrate the variety of interpretations offered to account for the distinctive patterns of American delinquency. Apart from the criticisms already applied to the anomie theory and which can also be applied to most of the subcultural approaches, the fact that the theories of Cohen, Cloward and Ohlin, and Miller offer very different and sometimes conflicting explanations for the same phenomena is in itself a major problem of the subculture approach. These theories were based on each author's personal observations, which were inevitably limited in scope; unfortunately, they were usually presented as definitive and universally applicable formulations, whereas the nature of their origins suggests that they should be treated as tentative hypotheses. None of them are characterized by a methodology that could be compared to the careful, empirical work of Thrasher and Whyte.

Nevertheless, they did give rise to a series of empirical studies in America that have tried to investigate, among other things, whether these theories were supported when subjected to more rigorous research study. The work of Gold (1963), who was concerned in part with Cohen's thesis, Spergel (1964), who investigated the Cloward and Ohlin typology, and Short and Strodtbeck (1965), whose study is relevant to all the theories mentioned, best illustrate through research practice the empirical difficulties of the concept of the subculture. At the empirical level these studies, and in particular the work of Short and Strodtbeck, suggest that the clearcut, neat explanations of the subcultural theorists do not adequately represent the complex processes leading to group delinquency. A main problem has been their almost exclusive concern with the structured gang; the available evidence, both American and English, suggests that the mass of delinquent acts are not committed by organized delinquent gangs but by small, fairly transient and loosely structured friendship groups; the role of the gang has thus been overemphasized in these theories. Similarly, only a tenuous commitment was found to specifically delinquent values, and those values that were espoused fairly consistently by official delinquents (for example, sexual prowess, being "cool" or "sharp") were not so much opposed to middle-class values, as Cohen suggested, but were rather alternatives to them. This empirical evidence fits in well with the most trenchant theoretical critique of the subcultural tradition, that of Matza (1964) in *Delinquency and Drift*. Matza's critique provides the link between the mainstream of delinquency theory, found in the notion of subculture and those writing from within the expanding interactionist perspective.

Matza argues that the subcultural theories suffered from one of the same faults as traditional criminology by presenting a highly deterministic view of the subcultural delinquent; each of the above, as well as other theories, implies that the childhood and adolescent male peer groups who commit a range of delinquencies are organized around the central value of delinquency and that the group members are fully committed to this value. The group and its main values and interests are pictured as being largely cut off and distinct from the ongoing conventional culture. Matza, in his own investigations, which are supported by Short and Strodtbeck's subsequent work, found that, far from this being the case, there was a distinct lack of commitment to specifically delinquent values. In fact, boys were often very ambivalent about their own delinquent activities and experienced guilt in relation to them; guilt would certainly not be present if the boys were fully committed to their delinquencies. Matza argues that the values that characterize delinquency, namely the search for excitement, a distaste for mundane hard work, and masculinity, are not specific to the delinquent subculture nor are they the antithesis of middle-class values; he suggests that, on the contrary, these values are distributed throughout the various social classes, but they emerge on different occasions and in different situations for different social groups. In the middle class, for example, these values typically emerge in the leisure situation, in sports or other ritual events. He calls this sharing of values "subterranean convergence;" these values, perhaps less respectable in the middle class, are kept below the surface for most of the time and only emerge in certain specially designated situations.

However, not only do the working-class boys' mundane delinquencies reflect badly timed extensions of commonly held values, but the delinquent can only be understood by recognizing that he is completely surrounded and dealt with by conventional culture and its various agents of social control. The delinquent subculture cannot therefore be viewed as cutoff, outside, or separate from the main body of society as earlier theorists had implied. Matza goes on to develop a thesis in which the mundane delinquent is seen in a situation of drift, committed neither to a conventional nor a deviant value system but flirting first with one, then with the other; the situation of drift is exacerbated by recurring features of the lower-working-class boys' social situation, especially by the long periods of boredom at school, home, and work, and by the extensive but empty periods of leisure. These often give rise to a mood of fatalism or desperation that facilitates the drift into delinquency.

Finally, Matza describes a series of common "techniques of neutralization" that the boys use to justify their delinquencies to themselves in particular circumstances while knowing them to be wrong. To free himself from the moral bind of the law that he recognizes most of the time, a boy uses special justifications or neutralizations that make the act right for him in that situation on that particular occasion. Calling these neutralizations of the bind of law into play allows him to commit the act with a relative lack of guilt feelings at the time. Without listing these techniques, it is sufficient to note that Matza goes back to the law itself to locate the neutralizations, for he argues that the delinquents' justification are but extensions of common, legitimate legal defenses; these defenses would normally lead to findings of innocence or at least to a lessening of the legal penalty by demonstrating that mitigating circumstances were present at the commission of the crime.

Matza thus attempts to escape from the determinism of subculture theory by proposing a theory of drift that draws attention to the total surrounding and penetrating of the working-class boy's culture by conventional culture and especially by agents of and beliefs about the legal system. From the deviance perspective, the four important features of his contribution are, first, its critique of sociological positivism or determinism; second, his stress on the similarity of and interaction between the culture of delinquency and the conventional culture; third, the introduction of aspects of social control agencies and especially the legal system as sources of the delinquents' justifications for their delinquencies; and finally, the role he gives to the meanings the delinquents themselves attach to their acts as providing the ultimate means to sociological understanding.

Emerging concerns in the analysis of delinquency

The empirical and theoretical shortcomings of the subcultural approach were increasingly realized as a result of some of the research undertaken in relation to delinquency, through Matza's critique and through the growing interest in the work of those writing from within an interactionist perspective who drew attention to fundamental problems not touched by the proponents of subculture. An early indication of this can be found in a study by Piliavin and Briar (1964) of police encounters with juveniles. Noting the immense latitude given to police officers in their decisions to formally arrest and charge juveniles or to deal with them less formally, they studied the features of the situation of encounter bctween police and juvenile suspects that influenced police officers' decisions on how to handle the cases. They concluded that the police had clear pictures or stereotypes of what they conceived to be basically "good" boys and serious troublemakers; they tended to base their offiical dispositions of the cases very much on these personal "theories" of what the "real" delinquent was like. The thing that influenced these stereotypes most strongly was the youths' demeanor, that is, how they dressed and especially how they behaved towards the officers, the uncooperative, aggressive youths being seen as the potential serious troublemakers and as the "real" delinquents. A later study by Skolnick (1966), concerned not specifically with juvenile delinquency but with the general social organization of the police and their processes of law enforcement, considers in much greater detail some of the issues raised by Piliavin and Briar and others by analyzing the relationships between the police and the community in one city.

The move away from the subcultural approach has been influenced and reinforced by the work of Cicourel. Heavily influenced himself by the social phenomenology of A. Schuetz, who saw the central task in sociology as the study of meaning structures, Cicourel's own work reflects a continuing concern with the relationship between theory and research in sociology. Apart from his main work on methodology (Cicourel, 1964), several of his most important contributions to sociology have been in the area of crime and delinquency. His influential early paper, written with Kitsuse, redefines the sociological uses of the official statistics; it was they who first proposed the argument discussed in the previous chapter, that official statistics must be viewed as indexes of official organizational activities and that one sociological task is to elucidate the meanings and activities through which the statistics were organizationally produced (Cicourel and Kitsuse, 1963a). The work of Piliavin and Briar is an example of a study that clarifies the processes of official record compilation by the police. In a further piece of research, again in collaboration with Kitsuse, Cicourel investigates the processes of decision-making in the school (Cicourel and Kitsuse, 1963b). Like the organizations in the penal system, the school can be seen as an organization producing various "official" rates such as a college-going rate, a truancy rate, or an early dropout rate; these and other rates reflect and are composed of different kinds of adolescent careers within the school such as the "high achiever," the "persistent truant," and the "unstable underachiever." The interest of Cicourel and Kitsuse is in how labels such as the above come to be attached to children in school and in the effects of the teachers' use of these labels on both the children and the various organizational rates. This kind of study, in seeing the school as an organization in which delinquent careers can emerge and produces, among other rates, a delinquency rate, has obvious relevance to the study of delinquency.

Cicourel's (1968) most recent study of how official files and statistics on juvenile delinquency are assembled in two cities is an extended investigation of his previous concerns. Comparing the two cities, Cicourel shows how particular features of the local police organization and policy led to different definitions of what constituted "the problem" of delinquency in the two communities; in their turn, these official definitions were reflected in the very different patterns of official statistics in the two otherwise comparable cities. Cicourel's work shows that the variance in official definitions of delinquency and what police officers consider relevant to their understanding of the problem and their dealings with those they define as delinquents should be treated as a basic problem for the researcher. From the interactionist perspective, the importance of these official definitions lies also in the ways in which they impinge on the official careers of delinquents, for, as suggested earlier, the nature of the deviant's contact with official agencies is one of the most important contingencies in the development of his deviant career; the outcome of the official definition is also reflected in the nature of the public stigma attached to the official offender. These are likely to vary as official definitions and actions vary. It is worth noting that this comprises only a part of Cicourel's contribution, for he is also concerned with issues of more general sociological interest, especially with those processes of negotiation and meaning construction through which members of a group endeavor to make sense of events in which they are involved by imposing commonly understood explanations on ambiguous features of these events. These explanations are invariably based on common-sense understandings or on what everybody in the society or social group is supposed to know and take for granted; it is these very taken-for-granted understandings that should be problematic for the sociologist. The latter must also attempt constantly to call into question his own assumptions about the phenomenon he investigates and the implicit rules he typically uses in interpreting these.

An analysis of the juvenile court complements Cicourel's wider study of juvenile justice. Emerson (1969) describes some features of the processes by which the court judges and manages delinquency cases; locating the court's concerns as the control of juvenile behavior and the prevention of serious delinquency, he finds these reflected in the court's procedure for identifying cases of "trouble" (those requiring special attention and measures of control). The assessment of "moral character" within the confines of the ceremonial structure of the court provides the basis for the decisions made; Emerson suggests that the court is a "reluctant labeler" whose authority backs up the authority of groups outside in the community. The court comes to share police standards of offense-severity and indexes of moral character with the result that "hard-core" cases are most likely to suffer incarceration and consequent reinforcing stigmatization.

It seems that the recent studies investigating delinquency from a stance more or less in harmony with an interactionist perspective have both widened and narrowed the focus of investigation. The focus has been widened by incorporating the study of the processes of social control, thereby raising questions that touch upon the fields of political sociology and the sociology of law. At the same time the focus has been narrowed by the attention it draws towards and the importance it vests in the structure of everyday common-sense meanings of those involved in the production of delinquency, including both those who commit certain acts and those who define this group as delinquent.

The relevance of American analysis to other cultures: England as an example

So far the discussion has been concerned exclusively with the developments in American sociological writing on delinquency, and these reflect both the practical and analytical concerns of American sociologists. Questions can be raised immediately concerning the relevance of these studies to the understanding of delinquency elsewhere. In terms of the content of American theories and studies, a distinction can be drawn between those aspects of the theories that refer to apparently universal social processes and those that refer to particular features of American society; those referring to general social processes, such as Cicourel's concern with the processes of statistical production, categorization, and social typing, would by definition seem to be more likely to provide useful data for cross-cultural comparisons than those referring to the substantive features of one society, such as Miller's discussion of the black family structure or Cloward and Ohlin's discussion of the retreatist subculture. Moreover, it is essential to remember that there are gross differences between American and, for example, English society that are closely related to some of the substantive features of American society held to be important in the various theories of delinquency.

Some of the more obvious differences are listed briefly; their relevance to features of the interactionist perspective will be clear. Comparing the social structures of American and English societies, there are major differences in the criminal laws of the two societies, for example, in relation to narcotics; there are major differences in the court and penal systems; police and judicial appointments are closely tied to local politics in the United States and are largely free of such ties in England; the educational system is differently organized at every level in terms of structure, content, and control; the ethnic structure of the two societies is completely different; the economic bases of the countries differ radically, as does the role of the central government in both the economic and welfare spheres; the actual pattern of physical violence, reflected in the different homicide rates, the private ownership of firearms and the use of firearms by the police is very different; and the role of organized labor in politics is very different in the two countries. All these things suggest that the meanings attached to the basic features of the individuals' social situations, especially to their class and status positions and to their aspirations and lifestyles, are also very different. With such gross and overt differences between the two societies in just those areas of fundamental importance to the various delinquency theories, it would be naive to expect that the simple transfer of an American theory to the English or other situations could make much of a contribution to our understanding of patterns of English delinquency. Such a transfer is more likely to mystify than to clarify.

In the only study that involves an attempt to investigate the relevance of American subcultural theory to the English situation, Downes (1966), in his research in East London, concluded that there was little evidence to support Cohen's reaction formation thesis, although there was some evidence for an "umbrella" or "parent" subculture with a variety of heterogeneous offsprings that was generally supportive of delinquency. There was even less evidence of Cloward and Ohlin's three types, although the subsequent rise in drug dependency among lower-working-class boys both in the area where he did his research and in other neighborhoods might require a modification of his conclusions on the retreatist response. Downes argued that a large group of inner urban working-class boys start off in a delinquency-prone life situation; dissociated from the values of school and later alienated from work, the boys indulge in occasional delinquencies as a peripheral leisure activity to manufacture excitement no longer provided by traditional working-class leisure culture. Downes thus saw delinquency as essentially hedonistic. However, his criticism of the American theories was presented in traditional terms, and he was not concerned directly with the issues and problems raised by the interactionist perspective; his methodology and restriction to one year's Metropolitan Police statistics, complemented by some informal discussion with older boys living in the area, clearly leaves much to be desired even by conventional standards.

Recent work by Hargreaves and Phillipson, focusing on the educational system, lends support to and provides useful background data on Cicourel and Kitsuse's analysis of the school as a rate- and career-producing institution. A study of 20 secondary schools in a London borough showed that they had very large and consistent differences in their official delinquency rates over a seven-year period; these differences could not be explained either in terms of the gross characteristics of the schools nor by differential police organization. Most importantly, it was found that the school rates were partially independent of the delinquency rates of their catchment areas; the high delinquency-rate schools did not draw their delinquent pupils disproportionately from high-rate neighborhoods and the low-rate schools from low-rate neighborhoods. Some schools seemed to be facilitating the drift into delinquency and others protecting their pupils from it (Phillipson, 1971). This finding is lent support by Hargreaves' (1967) study of one secondary school in which he describes the emergence of two kinds of subcultures in the school during the third and fourth years, one of which he describes as "delinquescent;" he shows how these two polar subcultures, one conforming to the values of the school and the other negating them, emerged as responses to features of the streaming system, the nature of the curriculum, and the types of interaction between teachers and pupils in the different streams. These two very different studies, together with Downes' discussion of working-class boys' dissociation from the school, point to the importance of subjecting the school to closer investigation in relation to its contribution to the production of delinquent careers.

Apart from Mayhew's vivid descriptions, very little sociological research into delinquency was undertaken in England until after World War II, and since that time there has been little on the same scale or of the same theoretical and methodological sophistication (admittedly sometimes misplaced) as the American work. There seem to be two complementary themes in the small number of studies carried out in England. First, there are those that have followed what may be loosely called a "neighborhood" perspective; these have focused on particular cities, towns or areas within them and have analyzed their broad socio-economic characteristics and the relationship of these to official patterns of delinquency and crime. Sometimes, as in the case of Mays' (1954) work in Liverpool, the focus has been more specifically on the character of delinquent activities of the boys within such areas. In addition to Mays' work, this group includes the studies of Mannheim (1948) in Cambridge, Jones (1958) in Leicester and Morris (1957) in Croydon; Morris' study also contains the best critique of the ecological tradition. Second, there are those studies that concentrated more on styles of family life in high delinquency neighborhoods and include the work of Sprott *et al.* (1954), Wilson (1962), Kerr (1958) and Spinley (1954), although the last two were only peripherally concerned with delinquency, and the work of Wilson is concerned with a very special group of "multi-problem" families.

These two broad types of studies converge and complement each other in their general conclusions. The stratum at the bottom of the social-class hierarchy seems to possess a culture with idiosyncratic characteristics; often described by the term "slum culture," one of its features is the general tolerance of a wide range of delinquencies, especially those relating to property. For boys living in such neighborhoods, the studies seem to suggest, that delinquency is defined as a "normal phenomenon," as something that everybody does. Family values and the character of family relationships in "slum culture" provide a supportive framework for the emergence of mundane and intermittent delinquent activities. At the most general level of comparison, the findings of these studies seem to be most akin to Miller's analysis in America.

No study has been concerned with social control processes, nor have there been any attempts in English research to investigate such things as the development of delinquent careers or the emergence of delinquent self-concepts; as English research in the past has very much taken its cues from developments in American thinking, it might be expected that increasing attention will be paid to those issues which are raised by the interactionist perspective. Because this perspective is concerned mainly with general social processes rather than with the specific features of a given society, it seems likely that, in spite of the fact that its main architects are American, its application to the study of delinquency in England and other societies will be more relevant than that of specific subcultural theories.

A final problem to be faced in generating theories that offer explanations of patterns of delinquency is particularly relevant in the English situation; this is the problem raised earlier of the ahistorical character of most theories. If some neighborhoods and communities have had high official delinquency rates for at least the past hundred years, as the evidence suggests, then how can sociologists come to terms with this in their interpretations? The problem is raised most acutely for those theories that place greatest emphasis on particular features of the total social structure; examples of the difficulties faced can be illustrated in the theories of Merton (1963) and Cohen (1955). Merton explains the high official rates of delinquency and crime among the lowest social-class groups as a common response to the situation of anomie, the disjunction between goals and legitimate means. One then has to ask at what stage in the society's history did this disjunction occur and for what reasons? Unless it has always been present in the same form, a most unlikely hypothesis, one must provide a different sort of explanation for delinquency and crime occurring prior to the emergence of the disjunction. Since there is this consistency in crime rates in some areas, one needs to know if delinquency and crime in the same neighborhoods change their meanings for the actors over time as a result of major structural changes. If so, what are these changes and how do they influence the meanings attached to delinquency?

The problem is even more pertinent to Cohen's theory, for he explicitly sets out to account for the *emergence* of the delinquent subculture, and as noted, he does this by seeing delinquency as a reaction formation response of working-class boys to their status frustration; this frustration is seen partly as a result of a conflict in values of two social classes. But a question Cohen does not consider is: When did this emergence of the subculture take place? When did the situation of working-class boys become so frustrating that delinquency was "discovered" as a solution? Again, one must ask if delinquency has changed its meaning for delinquent boys, for, as Bordua (1961) points out, Cohen's boys, driven to delinquency by status frustration, seem a far cry from Thrasher's boys, who found delinquency a positive source of excitement in an often dull and loosely controlled milieu. If delinquency has changed its meaning so drastically, one wants to know why; again Cohen gives us no clues as to the kind of major social changes that might have produced such changes in the meaning of delinquency. Not only is it very difficult to decide which social changes, if any, impinge on delinquent activity; it is even more difficult to spell out precisely the relationships between the phenomena and the nature of the influence.

Explanations of delinquency and crime in England face this problem in an acute way because of the very long-term consistency in the official delinquency rates of many neighborhoods. On the one hand, several explanations might be required, each related to a specific historical period; in each period delinquency, while running at approximately the same official rate and having the same character as the previous period, might mean different things to both the delinquents and the controllers; in taking this approach one would clearly have to explain what the changes in meaning were due to. On the other hand, one might offer a general theory that attempted to account for the historical continuity of the patterns and character of delinquency but tried to incorporate particular social changes into its explanation. If the meanings of delinquency for the community, including the regular delinquents, the occasional delinquents, the miniscule group of nondelinquents, and the social controllers (who may be delinquents too), have changed, the sociologist's task is to account for these changes by showing how, why, and when they occurred. Unfortunately the paucity of the kind of historical data necessary for such explanations makes this task very difficult and perhaps in part accounts for sociologists' failure in the past even to consider these issues.

6

Criminology, Sociology, Crime, and Social Policy

Introduction

This chapter discusses some of the implications for social policy of the distinctions made in the first two chapters between traditional criminology and the interactionist perspective. The underlying theme is the distinction between a social problem and a sociological problem. The study of crime and delinquency provides an excellent example of the confusions that have arisen in the social sciences over the relationship between social scientific theorizing and research activity, and social policy and political action. Here the stance is taken that a clear distinction can be made between social problems and sociological problems and that an understanding of this distinction is essential if the actual implications of sociological analysis for social action are to be brought to light. The following discussion draws heavily on Schuetz's (1967) analysis of common-sense and scientific modes of interpretation.

The distinction between practical and scientific projects

For the interactionist perspective, as for that general sociological perspective comprising the tradition of inter-

pretive understanding, the main methodological problem
is to achieve objective and verifiable knowledge of meaning-
structures. To understand how sociologists approach this
problem, a prerequisite is a clear picture of the way in
which the sociologist looks at the world and of the distinctive attitude he adopts towards it. Schuetz distinguishes
between what he calls the system of relevances characterizing man in his practical activities that arise within the
"natural attitude" and the system of relevances characterizing man in his role as scientist; in moving from the
natural attitude, which characterizes his stance towards
the nonscientific activities of his life and is the stance of
members of society in their everyday common-sense activities, to the scientific attitude, the social scientist detaches
himself from his biographical situation within the social
world. In using the term *system of relevances,* Schuetz is
referring to those elements of a social situation that the
actor, whether scientist or practical man, selects as relevant
to his project or his course of action; the term can thus be
defined and illustrated by the kinds of questions asked by
the actor in the course of his project that selectively orient
him to particular features within a situation. Schuetz's distinction between a scientific project and a practical project
of everyday living, includes the idea that the scientific project or problem, such as that of a sociologist, determines
what is relevant for the scientist; the orienting questions
which comprise the scientist's system of relevances are
quite different from the questions of the practical man. As
Schuetz says:

> The theoretical scientist—*qua* scientist, not *qua* human be-
> ing (which he is, too)—is not involved in the observed situa-
> tion, which is to him not of practical but merely of cognitive
> interest. The system of relevances governing common-sense
> interpretation in everyday life originates in the biographical
> situation of the observer. By making up his mind to become a

scientist, the social scientist has replaced his personal biographical situation by what I shall call . . . a scientific situation. The problems with which he has to deal may be quite unproblematic for the human being within the world and vice versa. Any scientific problem is determined by the actual state of the respective science and its solution has to be achieved in accordance with the procedural rules governing this science, which among other things warrant the control and verification of the solution offered. The scientific problem once established alone determines what is relevant for the scientist as well as the conceptual frame of references to be used by him (1967, p. 63).

This detachment of the scientist requires a move from involvement in practical activities to disinterested observation of them by the social scientist; the move from the natural attitude also requires him to suspend his belief in many of those things he had taken for granted within it. What was relevant for him in his biographical situation within the natural attitude is irrelevant to his problems as a scientist in the scientific attitude of suspended belief in the world previously taken for granted.

Of course, this suspension of belief in the world in the move from the natural attitude is an ideal for the sociologist to aim for rather than a description of what actually happens and is arguably the most difficult feature of the sociological project. As some aspects of his natural attitude inevitably enter into his scientific questions and decisions, the problem for the sociologist is to make explicit his system of relevances and to clarify his assumptions and decisions at every stage of his project. Unless this is done, it may be very difficult to evaluate his work, for many of the values out of which his conceptual and methodological decisions emerged will have remained implicit. The point that Schuetz is making is that the program for scientific research, that is, what the scientist investigates and how he investigates it, is determined by the scientific quest for certain kinds of truth, the validity and reliability of which are judged in terms of the criteria of scientific method; it is the system of relevances that characterizes the particular discipline of sociology, its concepts, assumptions, theories, and methods, that determines what is a problem for the sociologist and not the system of relevances of men in their natural attitudes facing practical problems of living. Schuetz then goes on to develop a program for sociological analysis within the scientific attitude and suggests what the main components of the social scientist's system of relevance might be. However, in this context it is sufficient to note that once the scientific problem has been established, it is this alone that determines what is relevant and what is not; in the scientific attitude the social scientist will tend to take for granted only those things accepted and established by his fellow scientists and those things deemed scientifically irrelevant to his scientific project in hand. If the scientific project shifts in character during the course of investigation, so accordingly does the system of scientific relevances; the different levels of scientific analysis each possess their own systems of relevances, each of which is quite distinct from systems of relevances characterizing the natural attitude.

The distinction between the formation and use of common-sense constructs and concepts—by means of which we describe and interpret our practical experiences in the natural attitude—and the constructs and concepts of science, further illustrates the difference between the scientific and the natural attitude. Our common-sense constructs arise out of our biographical situations and rest on and take for granted a stock of socially approved knowledge; these common-sense constructs have their place within the chains of motives characterizing the everyday activities of men. However, social scientific constructs and concepts are what

Schuetz calls "second-order constructs" and, as they arise
out of scientific problems, are very different from those
emerging in the natural attitude to deal with practical
problems. The stock of knowledge taken for granted by the
scientist is the knowledge that comprises his discipline and
includes a generally agreed body of concepts and methods
for forming scientifically useful concepts. What he takes for
granted as a scientist and what he calls into question are
quite independent of the accepted values, beliefs, and interests of men in their practical activities. If the main aim
of sociology is to achieve objective knowledge of meaning
structures, this task carries with it structures of relevances
and a stock of taken-for-granted scientific knowledge that
are inevitably completely different from those men bring to
bear on their practical activities in the world, for the latter's
aims arise out of their biographical situations. The world
would rapidly grind to a halt if men started in large numbers to adopt the social scientific attitude of suspension of
certain kinds of belief in their social worlds.

An illustration of the importance of this distinction can
be given by elaborating the comparison between traditional
criminology and the interactionist perspective. Some of the
main characteristics of the structures of relevances and
the stocks of taken-for-granted knowledge of the two perspectives can be contrasted with special reference to their
implications for practical action in relation to crime and
delinquency.

Criminology's system of relevances and stock of knowledge

In the critique of traditional criminology presented in
Chapter 1, particular stress was laid on its normative character; its subject matter was defined by criteria external
to the discipline, that is, by social definitions of what consti-

tuted crime and of the ways in which crime was a social problem requiring positive social action against it. Criminology was seen to be defined by and therefore inextricably bound up with society's definitions and problems; in effect, criminology was, and still is, the servant, first, of the political values that define crime and the criminal as immediately problematic for society and, second, of the personal values of the working criminologists, who broadly accept these political values and work within them and whose research work is directed to the practical everyday problems of penal systems.

The system of relevances characterizing criminology is congruent with that of politicians and members of society in their natural attitudes: Criminology shares with the public the common-sense definitions of crime and the criminal as major social problems. It does not suspend its belief in the socially shared assumptions about the pathological features of crime but accepts these assumptions and works within them; in so doing it allows these common-sense assumptions and definitions, which emerge from and lie within the natural attitude, to determine its problems of investigation. The problems addressed by criminology are handed to it by politicians and pressure groups or arise out of the personal values of the criminologists themselves within their natural attitudes and are not determined by a scientific system of relevances.

If this is the general structure of relevances within which criminologists operate, what are the typical components of their stock of taken-for-granted knowledge? Clearly, this knowledge, too, is largely nonscientific, for it lies within the structure of relevances just mentioned. The following seem to be the pervasive, implicit, and taken-for-granted assumptions in much criminological research and writing. Some of these assumptions are interrelated and are rarely found on their own but imply each other. First, there is the assumption that there are universal causes of crime that can be located through criminological research methods that in their turn rely heavily on the use and logic of the statistical method. This is closely related to another prime feature of criminology, namely, its division of the population into two groups, criminals, and noncriminals, the assumption being that the causes of crime can be located by finding factors that significantly differentiate the two groups. Third, and growing out of the first two assumptions, is the implicit notion in prescriptive criminological writing that if the causes of crime can be located by the study of individual criminals, the prevention of crime can best be achieved by doing something to these same individuals. Fourth, in analyzing patterns of crime in society, although lip service is generally paid to the limitations of official statistics as measures of the "problem," nevertheless they are still typically used as indexes of trends in crime.

An illustration of the difficulties of analysis these assumptions bring and which are typically not recognized by criminologists themselves can be found by a more detailed analysis of the third assumption concerning criminological views on crime prevention and the change of criminals. A common theme underlying the work of criminologists who investigate politically defined problems of the penal system is that of increasing its rationality by evaluating its activities; this rationality is defined in terms that attempt to relate limited penal ends to more effective means. For example, the main ends of the courts' sentencing activities are taken by criminologists, often quite explicitly, to be the reduction of recidivism, that is, preventing officially defined offenders from committing further crimes and deterring potential offenders; both Wootton (1963) and Wilkins (1965) propose this as the main aim of the sentencing process. Having accepted this as the main aim, criminologists typically proceed in their evaluative research as if it was the only aim of the penal system and develop techniques for measuring how effective court sentences and subsequent penal practices are in achieving this end with the processed offenders. The belief that presumably underlies this kind of research is that the evaluation techniques used will provide the society with better, more rational data on how its penal system is working and will enable it to make informed modifications of the system; findings from such investigations might lead eventually to political decisions affecting sentencing practice or changing the nature of penal regimes.

The assumption of a single main aim in the penal system on which such writings rest is such a simplification of the complexities of the ambiguous and conflicting ethical principles, justifications, and meanings underlying contemporary penal activities, that it grossly distorts the realities faced by courts and penal institutions. The distortion is more likely to confuse than to clarify practical actions within the penal system; insofar as the decisions and activities of penal institutions reflect other aims and meanings apart from the reduction of recidivism, such as retribution, protection of society or individual atonement, or insofar as they take on the symbolic meanings of punishment suggested in Chapter 3, the explicit limitation to a single aim in evaluative studies fails to come to terms with the actual meanings of penal activities.

The main implications for social policy of criminology's relevance structure and stock of taken-for-granted knowledge are politically comfortable and convenient. They suggest that the pursuit of criminological research and the implementation of changes in the penal system based upon its findings will bring an increased rationality into penal practices; the underlying assumption appears to be that this rationality will bring increasingly effective crime prevention and criminal treatment procedures. This optimistic view of the values of criminological research is likely to find general support among politicians and the public not only because it shares their definition of crime as a social problem but also because it poses no threat to existing social institutions and interest groups. The narrow views of causation and treatment imply that the problem can be effectively dealt with by minor modifications here and there to parts of the system, in particular by modifications of parts of the penal system. Thus, by taking for granted and working within societal definitions of the problem, criminology becomes a highly conservative and therefore politically convenient discipline, while criminologists themselves are servants of social policy who occasionally contribute to minor innovations in policy.

A word of caution is in order here. Although this may seem to be an indictment of criminology from a sociological standpoint, it is not intended to suggest that the presence of criminologists in the social policy-creating institutions cannot be reasonably justified in terms of conventional political values or that there are no aspects of criminological research that are of value to a society, such as providing it with more information about its practical penal problems. The important thing is rather to recognize the value bases of criminology and the implications of these for its wider claims both to scientific status and to providing the effective answers to a society's crime problem. Contemporary societies do justify the employment of criminologists, and their data is used in political decision-making; however, from a sociological perspective, their contributions must be judged according to criteria other than those used to justify criminology's narrow views of causation and treatment. For example, an important measure of their contribution would be how far their partial and limited view of rationality is accepted and acted upon in a given penal system and in what ways political decisions about the penal system are affected by the data criminologists produce.

Insofar as criminologists subscribe to a view of rationality in penal decision-making, however partial it is, and insofar as rationality is a tenet of humanism, as a group in the service of social policy criminologists can be viewed as a small humanizing force. Their role seems to be to recommend penal changes on the basis of a limited ethic of evaluation, and in doing this they contribute to the growth of certain kinds of rationality in social policy.

The interactionist perspective's system of relevances and stock of knowledge

The interactionist perspective contrasts markedly with traditional criminology both in its system of relevances and its stock of taken-for-granted knowledge; consequently it also carries with it different implications for social and penal policy. Its system of relevances, that is, its basic orienting questions about the phenomenon of crime, derives from its place in the sociological tradition of interpretive understanding. This broad tradition rests on assumptions about man and social life that have very particular conceptual and methodological implications, as was pointed out in Chapter 2. The interactionist perspective's problems are therefore defined not by societal definitions of what the problem is and what should be investigated but by a particular conceptual tradition in sociology. We have already seen that this tradition places the study of crime in the context of deviance from shared rules, emphasizes the interactional and dynamic character of social relations with its related focus on the interaction between rule-breakers and social controllers, and is methodologically founded on the study of structures of meaning. These comprise some of the main features of the interactionist perspective's system of relevances and indicate the kind of problems addressed by it. The orientation lays claim to certain kinds of objectivity and validity that are very different in character from those claimed by traditional criminology; the criteria of validity are derived from its techniques of concept formation, theory construction, and methods of investigation, all of which differ considerably from those of traditional criminology. In their discussions of sociological interpretations both Schuetz and Gibson Winter—whose concern is the relationship between social science, ethics, and social policy (Winter, 1966)—conclude that ultimately the validity of sociological interpretations must rest on there being direct continuity between the sociologist's models or interpretations (his "second-order constructs") and the lived experiences of the actors whose actions he is interpreting. Sociological interpretations must both make sense to and illumine the understanding of the actors studied by sociologists. The criteria of objectivity and validity in criminology rest largely on its adherence to narrow interpretations of statistical method, while the meaning of its explanations to those studies is never mentioned or recognized as a problem.

Methodologically the two approaches could hardly be further apart. In particular, the different ways they view the deviant or official offender are indicative of their polar systems of relevances. In traditional criminology, a deviant act is typically seen as a product or symptom of underlying causes that are multifactorial in character; the deviant act is rarely viewed as important in itself in terms of its meaning to its author, rather it is taken to be symptomatic of some underlying pathology. In the interactionist perspective exactly the opposite approach is followed, and the meaning of men's actions are in themselves the central concern of the sociologist. As Matza (1969) has pointed out in *Becoming Deviant,* the adoption of a correctional stance towards the deviant, which characterizes criminology and much earlier sociology, precludes the possibility of using one of the very methodological devices which is central to the interactionist perspective in its quest for interpretive understanding. This, very simply, is empathy, or the ability to take the role of the deviant or criminal effectively and see the world through his eyes. If a correctional stance is adopted, it becomes very difficult for the investigator to empathize with the deviant and to appreciate his meaning. The correctional stance thus reinforces the view that deviant acts are basically pathological because it maintains a distance between the criminologist and his subject which precludes empathy. Following Berger's (1968) suggestion that sociologists attempt to achieve "ecstasy" in their interpretations by dropping or standing outside their common-sense assumptions, so in attempting to understand the meaning of deviant acts must the sociologist suspend his conventional abhorrence or other emotion and attempt to take the deviant's perspective of the world. As Berger says, "Only by stepping outside the taken-for-granted routines of society is it possible for us to confront the human condition without comforting mystifications" (p. 171). In addition to the guides laid down by the scientific rules of procedure and the existing conceptual apparatus of the ongoing tradition, the other main feature of the sociological relevance system is the suspension of belief in common-sense values concerning the penal system. This involves a move from the natural attitude towards punishment and treatment to an attitude of radical doubt achieved through "ecstasy."

The components of the stock of taken-for-granted sociological knowledge that lie within its structure of relevances contrast markedly with those of traditional criminology and, like the latter's, are also interrelated. First, it is taken for granted that the content and pattern of crime and the responses to it are relative to time and place so that the search for universal causes is inappropriate: There may be common processes in very different societies, such as deviance from enforceable rules, attempts to control it, or public rituals for stigmatizing the deviant person, but the actual content of these processes will inevitably differ very considerably. Thus, while the sociologist will need to analyze the actual content of rules, their enforcement, and deviance from them within a society, if he is to provide a sociologically adequate interpretation of them, his main concern is to clarify sociological understanding of the social processes that are common to different societies. Second, the assumption, discussed in detail in Chapter 3, that crime and deviance and their punishment are normal phenomena in society and are fundamental features of social life, is central to sociological analysis of these phenomena. A recognition of normality again contrasts strongly with the natural attitude stance which views crime as inherently pathological and problematic. It also leads directly to a third taken-for-granted tenet—that crime cannot be eliminated from society. Indeed the direct implication of this for social policy is that all the preventive and treatment programs deriving from criminological research are doomed to failure; their failure rests, first, in their basic assumptions concerning the possibility of prevention and the viability of treatment and, subsequently, in the targets they choose for their preventive and treatment actions, that is, the limitation of their actions to officially designated offenders. A further assumption of the sociological perspective is that the common-sense measures of a society's patterns of crime and deviance, its official statistics, cannot be used for this purpose except in very isolated cases; official data are viewed as the product of a series of interactions between located offenders and social control agencies and as such they are to be seen as indexes of organizational behavior

rather than measures of deviance. These are some of the
main components of the stock of taken-for-granted sociological knowledge about crime and deviance: Placed in
their context of the sociological structure of relevances,
they direct sociologists' attention to very different analytical problems from those tackled by criminology.

The implications of this sociological stance towards its
subject matter are very different from those of traditional
criminology. From the viewpoint of criminology and the
natural attitude they are pessimistic and politically uncom-
fortable in their implication that radically to alter the pattern of crime in society would require fundamental and
large-scale changes in the social structure; simply tamper-
ing with isolated parts of the whole, as in the practices resulting from criminology, has no effect on patterns of crime
and criminality, for these are bound up with the essential
social processes and conditions of life characterizing a
society. Indeed, even if large-scale structural changes were
to occur and social relationships were radically reorgan-
ized, for whatever reasons, crime and deviance, being intrinsic to social organization, would not disappear but
would simply change their form; there would still be acts
defined as deviant and would still be attempts to control
them.

It must be made clear that these sociological assumptions
cannot in themselves be taken as support either for undertaking the kinds of changes required to alter the character
of crime or for maintaining the political status quo. They
simply represent a particular perspective towards the
phenomenon of crime, and the value conclusions drawn
from them by members of society in their natural attitudes
and by sociologists, too, when they return from the scientific to the natural attitude, will depend on their background
relevances and stocks of taken-for-granted social knowledge in their natural attitudes.

Sociological writing and social policy

If sociological problems are distinguishable from social problems by virtue of their origins in different relevance systems, can the relationship between sociological writing and research and problems of social policy be clarified? In terms of social policy the particular problem of crime is largely a problem of dealing with individual criminals and delinquents; although they may be discussed in more general terms in political debate, the everyday problems of the penal and welfare systems center on how to deal with particular individuals. The solutions to these practical problems emerge from the relevance systems of the natural attitude and include considerations of economic and political expedience, strongly felt moral beliefs and unarticulated taken-for-granted assumptions about the efficacy of punishment in changing and deterring offenders. A feature of sociology's relevance system, the fact that its theories, models and constructs are concerned with the *typical* features of action and meaning, immediately points up the problem of relating sociological conceptualization to the world of practical action. Sociological typifications of action and meaning, Schuetz's "second-order constructs," by definition are removed from the common-sense, practical activities of members of society; these typifications are a product of certain kinds of reflection by sociologists on the common-sense world. This would suggest that the main relationship between sociological reflection about the world and practical activities in the world lies, as Gibson Winter (1966) proposes, in sociology's ability to clarify these practical activities.

Insofar as sociological data and interpretations are valid, that is, insofar as they are accurate depictions from the standpoint of sociological abstraction of the way things are in the world, they do not, in themselves, support any common-sense interest or value position. Sociological evidence can be used to support the cases of those desiring social changes and those desiring to preserve the status quo because each group selects from sociological data that which supports its own case. An example of this can be found in the debate about the efficacy of capital punishment. Though sociologists have demonstrated that the murder rate of a society seems to be independent of its use of capital punishment, no study can deny or confirm that in a few cases it may have acted as a deterrent; nor can standard sociological measurement techniques for comparing and evaluating the deterrent effect of capital punishment deal with the conflicting desire for retribution held by many members of a society. The debate becomes, in the last analysis, one of clashing moral viewpoints in which sociological evidence can be used by both sides in the debate; obviously such evidence is most likely to appeal to those who in their natural attitudes share some of the assumptions of sociology. Perhaps only in those cases where a society claims to be doing one thing and actually acts in a way directly opposed to these claims can the sociologist act in some sense as the society's moral conscience. An illustration of this is Myrdal's *The American Dilemma* (1944), where he analyzes the contradictions between the fundamental American beliefs in freedom and equality and the social position of the black man in American society. The contribution of sociology, then, through its clarification of man's practical activities, is that it can help the members of a society to pose their own dilemmas more clearly and acutely.

With issues where there is overlap between sociologists' analytical interests and the common-sense societal definitions of a social problem, such as crime, mental health, or poverty, particular difficulties emerge for sociologists. Because there are important social problems, the sociologist whose work touches on such areas is subject to political pressures from interested groups that may try to influence both the content and the methods of his study. The sociologist's dilemma may be exacerbated by the fact that he often receives financial and other supports for his projects from groups that have a direct practical interest in the issues he investigates and the products of his research. In such situations the onus is placed on the sociologist to be as explicit as possible in his descriptions and explanations of his assumptions, his methodology, his concepts, and his findings simply because groups are likely to use his findings to support their own value interests. The sociologist's responsibility here is not only towards those who have helped to finance him but also, and more importantly, towards the people who have been the subjects of his investigation, for their lives may be changed as a result of the social uses of his research. In the case of those defined as deviant by the society, many changes in official policy may drastically affect their lives, so that sometimes the sociologist may feel it necessary to conceal certain sorts of information given to him in good faith by deviant characters. These dual and sometimes conflicting responsibilities can create considerable dilemmas for sociologists in the field of deviance and social problems.

A concluding point in relation to those dilemmas can be made in considering the relationship between the sociologist, his research findings, and his mundane membership of a society and his consequent engagement in its common-sense, practical activities. Whether the sociologist conducting a piece of research in an area also defined as a social problem decides to follow up through personal political action what he defines as the implications of his findings will depend on his personal values. The particular implications he selects for follow-up in personal action will rest not on his sociological knowledge but on his own view of the world in the natural attitude; in his common-sense perspective on the world, his sociological perspective is simply one among many interests and values, so his move from the scientific attitude back to the natural attitude brings back into play his common-sense understanding of the world and re-creates the background relevances necessary for his political action or inaction.

For Further Reading

The importance of placing the study of crime and delinquency in a general sociological context has been stressed throughout this book. It requires the investigator and the student to relate the substantive questions asked about crime to the general conceptual and methodological problems of sociology. Questions must be framed in terms of and placed within the context of sociological rather than social problems. Few sociologists working in the area of crime and delinquency have consistently made this distinction in their work, with the result that the bulk of written material on crime is "social problem" oriented. The reading recommendations made here are limited, with the exception of those relating to traditional criminology, to writers who tried to adopt a consistently sociological approach to the problems that interested them and whose work forms direct links with the mainstream of sociology.

The development of traditional criminology has been well documented from within by criminologists, the most comprehensive work being that of Mannheim (1965); in addition, Vold (1958) provides a succinct critique of the various "schools" of criminological explanation. The work of S. and E. Glueck (1950, 1964) epitomizes the methods and assumptions of traditional criminology, and one of their studies and a collection of their papers should give the flavor of their approach. Two articles by Tappan (1947) and Sellin (1938), reprinted in a book of readings (Wolfgang, Savitz and Johnston, 1962a), provide an early example of the debate between the traditional legalistic approach and the sociological orientation. A paper by C. Wright Mills (1963a) in which he criticizes the value assumptions of "social pathologists" was an early attempt to draw an analytical distinction between sociological and social problems.

Within the interactionist perspective there are very few writers who have contributed integrated and detailed approaches. Of these the most convincing and comprehensive is Lofland (1969), who presents a carefully documented conceptual approach to the analysis of deviance. Among the other contributions, Matza (1969), provides an excellent discussion of the emergence of the interactionist perspective within sociology, while Becker (1963, 1964) in his own book and in his introduction to a book of reading raises many of the issues and introduces some of the concepts that have been touched upon in this book. In his early work, Lemert (1951) first raised some of the ideas that are now taken for granted within the interactionist perspective and he himself elaborated subsequently (Lemert, 1967). More specifically, in relation to crime rather than deviance in general, Gibbons (1968) has presented an integrated approach to the study of criminality that centers on the concepts of role and career; many empirical studies that lend support to this approach can be found in Clinard and Quinney's (1967) book of readings. Examples of sociological approaches to other forms of social deviance can be found in Scheff's (1966) analysis of mental illness and Lindesmith's (1965) work on drug addiction.

Of the vast amount written on juvenile delinquency, mainly American, the following is a selection of the best of the theoretical and empirical work: the early "classics" of Thrasher (1927) and Shaw (1930, 1931) illustrate what can be gained from two contrasting methods, observation and studies of the delinquent career. Downes (1966) draws together the strands leading up to the subcultural approach and provides a detailed appraisal of American and English research. Matza's (1964) excellent critique of previous approaches to explaining delinquency and his own theory, together with Cicourel's (1968) study illustrate the movement to integrate the study of delinquency into general sociology. The researches of Short and Strodtbeck (1965) and Chein *et al.* (1964), in two contrasting fields of peer-group life, gang delinquency and drug use, illustrate the benefits of careful fieldwork.

More generally, the theoretical and methodological assumptions of this approach are most succinctly and lucidly presented by Schuetz in the essays contained in the first volume of his *Collected Papers* (1967); the papers in Part I of this volume present an excellent introduction to the perspective adopted in the present book. The implications of Schuetz's approach for general methodology in sociology are spelled out by Cicourel (1964), and in a more complex theoretical discussion, Gibson Winter (1966) surveys the relationship between different sociological perspectives and practical social action. Introductions to phenomenological sociology can be found in Douglas (1970a), and Filmer *et al.* (1972), while Garfinkel (1967) provides the foundations to which these introductions point.

The methodological style of observation, participant or otherwise, which is most appropriate to the interactionist perspective, is well illustrated by the studies of Whyte (1966), Liebow (1967) and Polsky (1967). Severyn Bruyn (1966) makes out the most convincing and persuasive case for this research style. The book of readings compiled by McCall and Simmons (1969) complements Bruyn's work, although many of the criticisms made by writers in this book are done from the standpoint of traditional methodology.

Readings

There is now an abundance of American readings in the fields of deviance and crime that brings together a wide range of papers and extracts from books. These readings inevitably reflect the personal tastes and interests of their compilers, so that any recommendation is somewhat arbitrary; moreover, because of the paucity of really good papers, there is often considerable overlap among the readings. However, apart from these limitations and the inevitable American bias of the books, the following have been carefully compiled and present some of the best papers written in the field of deviance.

CRESSEY, D. R. and WARD, D. A., eds (1969), *Delinquency, Crime and Social Process*, New York: Harper & Row.

DINITZ, S., DYNES, R. R., and CLARKE, A. C., eds. (1969), *Deviance*, London: Oxford University Press.

DOUGLAS, J. D., ed., "Deviance and Respectability," Basic Books, N.Y., 1970b.

DOUGLAS, J. D., ed., "Research on Deviance," Random House, N.Y., 1972.

DOUGLAS, J. D., ed., "Observations of Deviance," Random House, N.Y., 1970c.

LEFTON, M., SKIPPER, J. K., and MCCAGHY, C. H., eds. (1968), *Approaches to Deviance*, New York: Appleton-Century-Crofts.

RUBINGTON, E. and WEINBERG, M. S., eds. (1968), *Deviance: the interactionist perspective*, New York: Macmillan.

Specifically in the field of delinquency Giallombardo's book contains a wide range of material:

GIALLOMBARDO, R., ed. (1966). *Juvenile Delinquency*, New York: John Wiley.

The Harper Row "Social Problems" series contains a collection of shorter books of readings on particular types of social deviance such as mental illness, alcoholism, narcotic addiction, and middle-class juvenile delinquency.

Books of readings dealing specifically with the English situation from an explicitly sociological perspective are:

WILES, P. and CARSON, W. G., eds. (1971), *Crime and Delinquency in Britain: Sociological Readings*, London: Martin Robertson.

COHEN, S. ed. "Images of Deviance," Penguin, London, 1971.

The interests of traditional criminology are represented by:

British Journal of Criminology
Journal of Criminal Law, Criminology, and Police Science

Sociological papers on crime and delinquency are much more widely scattered across the range of American and English sociology journals. However, two journals are of special importance in this area; the main focus of the American journal *Social Problems* is the field of social deviance, and it contains a wide range of articles and research reports relating to this area; another American journal, *Social Forces*, although more wide-ranging in its sociological subject matter, frequently contains articles in the field of social deviance.

Bibliography

AUBERT, V. and S. MESSINGER, 1958. The criminal and the sick. *Inquiry* 1 : 37; FRIEDSON, E., and LORBER, J., eds. 1972. *Medical Men and Their Work*. Chicago: Aldine.

BECKER, H. S. 1963. *Outsiders: Studies in the Sociology of Deviance*. New York: Free Press.

————, ed. 1964. *The Other Side*. New York: Free Press.

BERGER, P. 1968. *Invitation to Sociology*. London: Penguin Books.

BERNSTEIN, B. 1960. Language and social class. *British Journal of Sociology* 11 : 271–76.

BITTNER, E. 1967. The police on skid row. *American Sociological Review* 32 : 715.

BLUM, A. 1970. The sociology of mental illness. In *Deviance and Respectability*, ed. J. Douglas. New York: Basic Books.

BLUMBERG, A. 1967. *Criminal Justice*. Chicago: Quadrangle.

BORDUA, D. 1961. Delinquent subcultures: sociological interpretations of gang delinquency. *Annals of the American Academy of Political and Social Science* 338 (November) : 119–36. Reprinted in Wolfgang, Savitz and Johnston, eds. 1962.

————, ed. 1967. *The Police: Six Essays*. New York: Wiley.

BRUYN, S. T. 1966. *The Human Perspective in Sociology*. Englewood Cliffs, N.J.: Prentice-Hall.

BURGESS, E. 1942. "Introduction" in Shaw, C. R. and McKay, H. D. *Juvenile Delinquency and Urban Areas*. Chicago: University of Chicago Press.

195

CAMERON, M. O. 1970. The five finger discount. In Smigel, E. O. and Ross, H. C., eds. 1970.

CARLIN, J. E. 1966. *Lawyers' Ethics.* New York: Russell Sage Foundation.

CHAPMAN, D. 1968. *Sociology and the Stereotype of the Criminal.* London: Tavistock.

CHEIN, I., D. L. GERARD, R. S. LEE, and E. ROSENFELD. 1964. *The Road to H.* London: Tavistock.

CHRISTIE, N. 1968. Changes in penal values. In N. Christie, ed. 1968. *Aspects of Social Control in Welfare States.* London: Tavistock.

CICOUREL, A. V. 1964. *Method and Measurement in Sociology.* New York: Free Press.

———. 1968. *The Social Organization of Juvenile Justice.* New York: Wiley.

CICOUREL, A. V., and J. I. KITSUSE. 1963 (a). A note on the use of official statistics. *Social Problems* 11 (Fall) : 131–39.

———. 1963 (b). *The Educational Decision Makers.* Indianapolis: Bobbs-Merrill.

CLEMMER, D. 1958. *The Prison Community.* New York: Rinehart.

CLINARD, M. ed. 1964. *Anomie and Deviant Behavior.* New York: Free Press.

CLINARD, M. and R. QUINNEY, eds. 1967. *Criminal Behavior Systems.* New York: Holt, Rinehart and Winston.

CLOWARD, R. and L. OHLIN. 1960. *Delinquency and Opportunity.* Chicago: Free Press.

COHEN, A. 1955. *Delinquent Boys.* Chicago: Free Press.

———. 1966. *Deviance and Control.* Englewood Cliffs, N.J.: Prentice-Hall.

CONRAD, J. 1965. *Crime and its Correction.* London: Tavistock.

CRESSEY, D. 1953. *Other People's Money.* Chicago: Free Press.

CRESSEY, D. and J. IRWIN. 1964. Thieves, convicts and the inmate culture. In H. Becker. ed. 1964.

DOUGLAS, J. ed. 1970 (a). *Understanding Everyday Life.* Chicago: Aldine.

———. 1970 (b). *Deviance and Respectability.* New York: Basic Books.

————. 1970 (c). *Observations of Deviance*. New York: Random House.

————. 1972. *Research on Deviance*. New York: Random House.

DOWNES, D. M. 1966. *The Delinquent Solution*. London: Routledge and Kegan Paul.

DURKHEIM, E. 1950. *The Rules of Sociological Method*. Chicago: Free Press.

————. 1951. *Suicide*. Chicago: Free Press.

————. 1961. *Moral Education*. New York: Free Press.

————. 1965. *Division of Labour*. New York: Free Press.

DUSTER, T. 1969. In S. Plog and R. Edgerton. *Changing Perspectives in Mental Illness*. New York: Holt, Rinehart and Winston.

EMERSON, R. 1969. *Judging Delinquents*. Chicago: Aldine.

ENNIS, P. H. 1967. *Criminal Victimization in the United States*. Washington: U.S. Government Printing Office.

ERIKSON, K. T. 1962. Notes on the sociology of deviance. *Social Problems* (Spring) : 307–14. In Becker. ed. 1964.

FILMER, P., M. PHILLIPSON, D. SILVERMAN, and D. WALSH. 1972. *New Directions in Sociological Theory*. London: Collier Macmillan.

FRIEDLANDER, K. 1947. *The Psychoanalytic Approach to Juvenile Delinquency*. New York: International Universities.

GARFINKEL, H. 1956. Conditions of successful degradation ceremonies. *American Journal of Sociology* LXI: 420–24.

————. 1967. *Studies in Ethnomethodology*. New York: Prentice-Hall.

GARFINKEL, H. and H. SACKS. 1970. On formal structures of practical action. In J. McKinney and E. Tiryakian. eds. 1970. *Theoretical Sociology*. New York: Appleton, Century, Crofts.

GENET, J. 1964. *The Thief's Journal*. New York: Grove.

GERTH, H. H. and C. W. MILLS. 1961. *Character and Social Structure*. London: Routledge and Kegan Paul.

GIALLOMBARDO, R. 1966. *Society of Women*. New York: Wiley.

GIBBONS, D. 1968. *Society, Crime and Criminal Careers*. Englewood Cliffs, N.J.: Prentice-Hall.

GLASER, D. 1964. *The Effectiveness of a Prison and Parole System*. Indianapolis: Bobbs-Merrill.

GLOVER, E. 1960. *The Roots of Crime*. London: Imago.

GLUECK, S. and E. 1950. *Unravelling Juvenile Delinquency*. Cambridge, Mass.: Harvard University.

———. 1964. *Ventures in Criminology*. London: Travistock.

GOFFMAN, E. 1961. *Asylums*. Chicago: Aldine.

———. 1963. *Behavior in Public Places*. New York: Free Press.

GOLD, M. 1963. *Status Forces in Delinquent Boys*. Ann Arbor: University of Michigan.

GUSFIELD, J. 1963. *Symbolic Crusade*. Urbana: University of Illinois.

HALL, J. 1939. *Theft, Law, and Society*. Indianapolis: Bobbs-Merrill.

HARGREAVES, D. 1967. *Social Relations in a Secondary School*. London: Routledge and Kegan Paul.

HARRÉ, R. and P. SECORD. 1972. *The Explanation of Social Behavior*. Oxford: Blackwell.

HAZELRIGG, L. ed. 1968. *Prison Within Society*. New York: Anchor.

HOME OFFICE. 1967. *Criminal Statistics for England and Wales*. London. H.M.S.O.

———. 1969. ——————————————————.

IRWIN, J. 1970. *The Felon*. Englewood Cliffs, N.J.: Prentice-Hall.

JACKSON, G. 1970. *Soledad Brother*. London: Penguin.

JONES, H. 1958. Approaches to an ecological study. *British Journal of Delinquency* VIII (.4) : 277–93.

KERR, M. 1958. *The People of Ship Street*. London: Routledge and Kegan Paul.

KOBRIN, S. 1959. The Chicago Area Project. *Annals of the American Academy of Political and Social Science* 322 (March): 20–29.

KUHN, T. 1970. *The Structure of Scientific Revolutions*. Chicago: University of Chicago.

LEMERT, E. 1951. *Social Pathology*. New York: McGraw-Hill.

———. 1958. The behavior of the systematic cheque forger. *Social Problems* 6 (Fall) : 141–49.

———. 1967. *Human Deviance, Social Problems, and Social Control*. Englewood Cliffs, N.J.: Prentice-Hall.

LEVINE, M. L., G. C. MCNAMEE, and D. GREENBERG. 1970. *Tales of Hoffman*. New York: Bantam.

LIEBOW, E. 1967. *Tally's Corner*. Boston: Little, Brown.

LINDESMITH, A. 1965. *The Addict and the Law*. New York: Vintage.

LINDESMITH, A., and Y. LEVIN. 1937. The Lombrosian myth in criminology. *American Journal of Sociology* XLII (March): 653–71.

LOFLAND, J. 1969. *Deviance and Identity*. Englewood Cliffs, N.J.: Prentice-Hall.

MC CALL, G. J., and J. L. SIMMONS. eds. 1969. *Issues in Participant Observation*. Reading, Mass.: Addison-Wesley.

MC CORD, W. and J. 1959. *Origins of Crime: a new evaluation of the Cambridge-Somerville Youth Study*. New York: Columbia University.

MALCOLM X. 1964. *Autobiography of Malcolm X*. New York: Grove.

MANNHEIM, H. 1948. *Juvenile Delinquency in an English Middletown*. London: Kegan Paul, Trench, and Trubner.

———. 1965. *Comparative Criminology* Vols. I and II. London: Routledge and Kegan Paul.

MANNHEIM, H. and L. WILKINS. 1955. *Prediction Methods in Relation to Borstal Training*. London: H.M.S.O.

MARTIN, J. P. 1962. *Offenders as Employees*. London: Macmillan.

MATHIESEN, T. 1965. *The Defences of the Weak*. London: Tavistock.

MATTHEWS, A. R. 1970. *Mental Disability and the Criminal Law*. Chicago: American Bar Foundation.

MATZA, D. 1964. *Delinquency and Drift*. New York: Wiley.

———. 1969. *Becoming Deviant*. Englewood Cliffs, N.J.: Prentice-Hall.

MAYHEW, H. 1862. *London Labour and the London Poor* Vol. IV. Edited and published as, *London's Underworld*. London: Spring Books. 1966.

MAYS, J. B. 1954. *Growing Up in the City*. Liverpool: Liverpool University Press.

MEAD, G. H. 1918. The psychology of punitive justice. *American Journal of Sociology* XXIII: 577–602.

———. 1934. *Mind, Self and Society*. Chicago: University of Chicago Press.

MERTON, R. K. 1963. *Social Theory and Social Structure*. New York: Free Press.

MILLER, W. B. 1958. Lower class life as a generating milieu of gang delinquency. *Journal of Social Issues*. XIV (no. 3): 5–19.

———. 1962. The impact of a total-community delinquency control project. *Social Problems* X (Fall): 168–91.

MILLS, C. W. 1963 (a). The professional ideology of social pathologists. In *Power, Politics and People*. New York: : Oxford University Press.

———. 1963 (b). Situated actions and vocabularies of motive. In *Power, Politics and People*. New York: Oxford University Press.

MINTON, R. ed. 1971. *Inside*. New York: Random House.

MORRIS, T. 1957. *The Criminal Area*. London: Routledge and Kegan Paul.

MORRIS, T. and P. 1963. *Pentonville*. London: Routledge and Kegan Paul.

MORRISON, A. 1896. *A Child of the Jago*. Reprinted, London: Penguin Books. 1946.

MYRDAL, G. 1944. *An American Dilemma*. New York: Harper.

NEWMAN, D. 1962. Pleading guilty for considerations. In M. Wolfgang, L. Savitz and N. Johnston. 1962.

O'NEILL, J. 1972. *Sociology as a Skin Trade*. London: Heinemann.

PARK, R. E., with E. W. BURGESS, R. D. MACKENZIE, and L. WIRTH. 1925. *The City*. Chicago: University of Chicago Press.

PHILLIPSON, C. M. 1971. Juvenile delinquency and the school. In P. Wiles and W. G. Carson. eds. 1971. *Crime and Delinquency in Britain*. London: Martin Robertson.

PILIAVIN, I. and S. BRIAR. 1964. Police encounters with juveniles. *American Journal of Sociology* LXX (Sept.): 206–14.

PLATT, A. 1969. *The Child Savers*. Chicago: University of Chicago Press.

POLSKY, N. 1967. *Hustlers, Beats and Others*. Chicago: Aldine.

POWER, M. J. 1962. Trends in juvenile delinquency. *The Times*. 9th August.

————. 1965. An attempt to identify at first appearance before the courts those at risk of becoming persistent juvenile offenders. *Proceedings of Royal Society of Medicine* LVII (No. 9) : 704–05.

PRESIDENT'S COMMISSION ON LAW ENFORCEMENT AND THE ADMINISTRATION OF JUSTICE. 1967. (a). *Task Force Report: Corrections.* Washington: U.S. Government Printing Office.

————. 1967 (b). *The Challenge of Crime in a Free Society.* Washington: U.S. Government Printing Office.

ROBIN, G. D. 1970. The corporate and judicial disposition of employee thieves. In E. O. Smigel and H. C. Ross. eds. 1970.

RUSCHE, G. and O. KIRCHEIMER. 1930. *Punishment and Social Structure.* New York: Columbia University Press.

SACKS, H. 1972. In D. SUDNOW, ed. *Studies in Interaction.* New York: Collier Macmillan.

SARTRE, J-P. 1963. *Saint Genet.* New York: Mentor.

SAVITZ, L. 1967. *Dilemmas in Criminology.* New York: McGraw-Hill.

SCHEFF, T. J. 1966. *Being Mentally Ill.* Chicago: Aldine.

SCHRAG, C. 1954. Leadership among prison inmates. *American Sociological Review* 19: 37.

SCHUETZ, A. 1967. *Collected Papers* Vols. I-III. The Hague: Martinus Nijhoff.

SCHUR, E. M. 1965. *Crimes Without Victims.* Englewood Cliffs, N.J.: Prentice-Hall.

SCOTT, M. and S. LYMAN. 1968. Accounts. *American Sociological Review.* 33: 46.

SELLIN, T. 1938. *Culture, Conflict and Crime.* New York: Social Science Research Council, Bulletin 71: 17–32.

SHAW, C. R. 1930. *The Jack Roller.* Chicago: University of Chicago Press.

————. 1931. *The Natural History of a Delinquent Career.* Philadelphia: Albert Saifer.

SHAW, C. R. and H. D. MCKAY. 1942. *Juvenile Delinquency in Urban Areas.* Chicago: University of Chicago Press.

SHORT, J. F. and F. L. STRODTBECK. 1965. *Group Process and Gang Delinquency.* Chicago: University of Chicago Press.

SKOLNICK, J. H. 1966. *Justice Without Trial.* New York: Wiley.
——. 1969. *The Politics of Protest.* New York: Ballantyne.
SMIGEL, E. O. and H. C. ROSS. 1970. *Crimes Against Bureaucracy.* New York: Van Nostrand.
SPERGEL, I. 1964. *Racketville, Slumtown, and Haulberg.* Chicago: University of Chicago Press.
SPINLEY, B. 1954. *The Deprived and the Privileged.* London: Routledge and Kegan Paul.
SPROTT, W. J. H., P. JEPHCOTT, and M. CARTER. 1954. *The Social Background of Delinquency.* University of Nottingham (unpublished).
STINCHCOMBE, A. 1963. Institutions of privacy in the determination of police administrative practice. *American Journal of Sociology* LXIX: 150–60.
STOLL, C. 1968. Images of man and social control. *Social Forces* 47 (no. 2): 119–27.
SUDNOW, D. 1965. Normal Crimes. *Social Problems* 12 (Winter): 255.
——. ed. 1972. *Studies in Interaction.* New York: Collier Macmillan.
SUTHERLAND, E. H. 1949. *White Collar Crime.* New York: Holt, Rinehart, Winston.
SUTHERLAND, E. H. and D. CRESSEY. 1960. *Principles of Criminology.* New York: Lippincott.
SYKES, G. 1958. *The Society of Captives.* Princeton: Princeton University Press.
SYKES, G. and S. MESSINGER. 1965. The inmate social system. In, *Theoretical Studies in the Organization of the Prison.* New York: Social Science Research Council.
TANNENBAUM, F. 1938. *Crime and the Community.* Boston: Ginn.
TAPPAN, P. 1947. Who is the criminal? *American Sociological Review* (Feb.): 12.
THOMAS, W. I. 1966. *On Social Organization and Personality.* Chicago: University of Chicago Press.
THRASHER, F. M. 1927. *The Gang.* Chicago: University of Chicago Press.
TOBIAS, J. J. 1967. *Crime and Industrial Society in the Nineteenth Century.* London: Batsford.

VOLD, G. B. 1958. *Theoretical Criminology*. New York: Oxford University Press.

WALKER, N. 1965. *Crime and Punishment in Great Britain*. Edinburgh: Edinburgh University Press.

———. 1967. A century of causal theory. In H. Klare and D. Haxby. eds. *Frontiers in Criminology*. London: Pergamon.

WALLERSTEIN, J. S. and C. WYLE. 1947. Our law-abiding law breakers. *Probation* 25:107–12.

WARD, D. and G. KASSEBAUM. 1965. *Woman's Prison*. Chicago: Aldine.

WARREN, C. 1972. Observing the gay community. In J. Douglas. ed. 1972.

WEBER, M. 1949. *The Methodology of the Social Sciences*. Chicago: Free Press.

WHYTE, W. F. 1966. *Street Corner Society*. Chicago: University of Chicago Press.

WIEDER, L. 1969. *The Convict Code*. Unpublished Ph.D. thesis. University College Los Angeles.

WILKINS, L. 1964. *Social Policy, Action, and Research*. London: Tavistock.

———. 1965. Evaluation of penal treatments. In P. Halmos. ed. 1965. *Sociological Studies in the British Penal Services*. Keele: Keele University Press.

WILSON, H. 1962. *Delinquency and Child Neglect*. London: Allen and Unwin.

WINTER, G. 1966. *Elements for a Social Ethic*. New York: Macmillan.

WIRTH, L. 1964. *On Cities and Social Life*. Chicago: University of Chicago Press.

WOLFGANG, M., L. SAVITZ, and N. JOHNSTON. eds. 1962. *The Sociology of Crime and Delinquency*. New York: Wiley.

WOLFGANG, M. and F. FERRACUTI. 1967. *The Sub-culture of Violence*. London: Tavistock.

WOOTTON, B. 1963. *Crime and the Criminal Law*. London: Stevens.

YABLONSKY, L. 1967. *The Violent Gang*. London: Penguin Books.

Index

205

UNDERSTANDING CRIME AND DELINQUENCY
BY MICHAEL PHILLIPSON

Publisher / Alexander J. Morin
Production Editor / Nanci Oakes Connors
Production Manager / Mitzi Carole Trout

Designed by Aldine Staff
Composed by Typoservice Corporation,
Indianapolis, Indiana
Printed and Bound by George Banta Company, Inc.
Menasha, Wisconsin